C000220687

# HOW TO BE A MINISTER

# HOW TO BE A MINISTER

## A 21ST-CENTURY GUIDE

JOHN HUTTON & LEIGH LEWIS

First published in Great Britain in 2014 by
Biteback Publishing Ltd
Westminster Tower
3 Albert Embankment
London SE1 7SP


ISBN 978-1-84954-732-1

10 9 8 7 6 5 4 3 2 1

A CIP catalogue record for this book is available from the British Library.

Set in Chaparral Pro

Printed and bound in Great Britain by
CPI Group (UK) Ltd, Croydon CR0 4YY

# CONTENTS

# FOREWORD

MOST BOOKS HAVE A SINGLE author. Ours has two. How we came to decide to write down together some of our experiences of government in the way we have here is a story for another day. But it raised the question of how we should try to do it. A book in two halves? Alternating 'his and hers' chapters – though in our case 'his and his'? Highlighted sections within chapters in each of our names?

In the end – though we have used the last two of these devices for some of our chapters – we've opted for the most part not to try and identify precisely which of us wrote what. That is not least because the more we worked together the more the product became an amalgam of us both and the more it became increasingly artificial to try to keep our contributions entirely separate. Sometimes it is still explicit, or at least pretty obvious, which of us wrote what. In other cases the forensically minded reader, or the reader who knows us both, will be able to work out at least who did the first draft. And although we burned the midnight oil as we approached the end of our work to try and make our two styles more consistent we have not been entirely successful.

But we don't apologise too much for this lack of uniformity. With only the rare exception we do agree on all of the key themes and conclusions we have drawn out. And if the net result is still a bit uneven in places – despite the best efforts of our editor – then that reflects rather well on the nature of government, which is very rarely neat, simple or clear. We hope that our readers will thus forgive us our inconsistencies.

On one thing, however, there is no inconsistency, namely the fact that we have drawn shamelessly on the advice, recollections and views of many of our present and former colleagues in government – both when they knew we were doing so and, very often, when they didn't – in the process of writing this volume. In general they are far too numerous for us to be able to thank them all individually though we unreservedly do so collectively.

There are, though, two exceptions deserving of special mention. The first is Mark Neale, a former senior civil servant and colleague at the Treasury, Home Office and DWP who gave up many hours to read emerging sections of our work and made many thoughtful and helpful suggestions. The second is James Purnell, a hugely valued friend and colleague to us both, who was a driving force in helping us initiate and complete our work. Needless to say, however, the resulting work, including all of its errors and imperfections, is ours and ours alone.

John Hutton and Leigh Lewis
London, July 2014

# PART I

## THE FAILSAFE GUIDE TO HOW TO BE A MINISTER – AND HOW TO RESIGN IF IT FAILS

## CHAPTER 1

# I'M HERE TO MAKE A DIFFERENCE

*Chi Wen Tzu always thought three times before taking action. Twice would have been quite enough.*

CONFUCIUS (C550–478BCE)

ALL MINISTERIAL CAREERS MAY END in failure, but they all start in hope. Not everyone thinks they're heading to No. 10 (though far more travel in hope than arrive, or were really sensible to think they might).

But everyone wants to do something. Politics has all sorts of downsides – but it has one unique upside: if you're lucky and become a minister you are handed a set of decision levers that are attached to something – when you pull on them something quite remarkable can happen. You can prevent or win wars. You can reduce poverty. You can create the NHS or, just sometimes, you can prevent real injustice.

Those rare days when you are first appointed or promoted should be treasured. There will not be many of them so savour each one as it comes along. But, as you stride purposefully through the ministerial floor for the very first time, trying to look confident and bashful at the same time, do take a couple of seconds to notice the row of photographs hanging outside your office. They start in black-and-white and edge into colour for the last few. Some you recognise immediately, some you are embarrassed to discover were Secretaries of State from your party's previous administration, whose existence you had forgotten.

They are your predecessors. All of them made this walk for the first time. And all of them made it for the last time too. So will you.

Ask yourself: for how many of them, can you remember anything they did? Sure, if you sought them out now in their city boardroom or Antipodean University, they could list all the great achievements they remember from their time in office. But could anyone else list them?

Yes, I know, politics can be a pretty grim life, but stop complaining – no one is ever going to sympathise. Instead, try to do something meaningful with your time in office. You're lucky to be here at all – many aspiring MPs never even make it to Parliament. Many aspiring front-benchers never catch the eye of their leader. And many opposition parties never make it into government.

You have cleared all these hurdles; this is payback time. Christopher Hitchens says that friends are what God gives us to apologise for relatives. Well, office is what God gives us to apologise for website comments at the bottom of that seminal article you wrote for 'Comment is Free'. Or for having to share your sleeper cabin to Glasgow with a loquacious constituent returning from a well-lubricated business conference in London.

So, don't just ring your Mum and Dad from your new ministerial telephone – though don't forget to do that; they are unbelievably proud of you. Work out quickly what it is you're going to do as a minister.

Not a bad place to start is to think how to start. As the 1980s TV series *Howards' Way* so accurately said: you never get a second chance to make a first impression. The public don't pay much attention to politics, and have quite a short attention span, though often longer than the political journalists through whom they find out about politics.

To be fair to Lobby journalists (not something many ministers can do after the first few weeks in office), they have to cover every department in Whitehall and all the political parties. All you have to do is understand your own department. They can be forgiven for not knowing the ins and outs of the Child Support Agency, or that its name has been changed to CMEC.

You need to make it easy for them. You need to give them a frame in which they can put you. They will quickly caricature you, unless you do it for them first.

So, what are you going to be: tough on welfare or the champion of the poor? Public service reformer or defender of the public service ethos? Intervening before breakfast, lunch and dinner; or the scourge of *Rip Off Britain*? The iron chancellor or the great spender?

Yes, I know, you can be tough on welfare so as to help the poor. You can be prudent so as to spend later. You can intervene in industry while having a tough competition policy. And you can both support public service as well as champion the contribution that the outsourcers can bring to the table.

But if you go for a frame of reference that no one understands, then you may as well not have tried.

Here's a simple test. You'll have received a letter from a Lobby journalist who was always too grand for you, but who has suddenly decided to ask you out for lunch. The first course will be gossip. Then over the second course, they'll feel a duty to ask you what you want to do with your department. If they're pushing their peas around the plate after a couple of minutes, then your frame is too complicated.

Or, put another way, you can only be one thing. This is what is called definition. It means standing for something. If you don't, you may as well just enjoy the dinners and concentrate on making some good contacts for your post-ministerial career. Because without definition, your civil servants won't know what you want them to do, and if by some miracle you still manage to get something done, the public won't have noticed you've done it.

Definition is the opposite of triangulation. Triangulation is the art of making yourself sound reasonable by contradistinction against exaggerated opposites. For example: 'Old Labour would never sack any teachers, however bad: the Tories would have to fire lots of good teachers: we would pay properly the good teachers and get rid of the bad ones.'

Triangulation can work in opposition. It sounds reasonable, allows you to tell voters why you're no longer the party that they ejected from government a few years ago (an important pathway to getting back to power) while categorising the new government as extreme or failed.

But triangulation has a small problem: it usually leads to disaster in government. It leads to a desire to support both sides of an argument at the same time, to avoid decisions which have any downsides and never to make enemies. Ever. And that leads to a simple place: stasis, at which point you should start brushing up those headhunter contacts again.

But how do you work out what you want to do? Ideally, you've been put in a department that you know something about. Getting this is slightly tricky, because it's also rather badly seen in No. 10 to lobby for a particular ministerial job. Any minister who keeps on appearing in the press as desperate to be Foreign Secretary is rather more likely to end up in Agriculture. Nor is it much less embarrassing to keep on button-holing the Political Secretary, the head of the Policy Unit, the Chief Whip, the Prime Minister's wife, Rita the tea lady, about how really the current Education Secretary is making a horrible mess of things.

No, the best you can really hope for is to develop an expertise and have it noticed. Get yourself appointed to a Select Committee. Have a policy idea. Write a chapter of a set of essays. Get an article in the *FT* – or on 'Comment is Free' if the *FT* won't have you. If anyone from No. 10 does ever ask you what job you'd like, be honest, modest, but nonchalant (if you can manage it).

Let's assume you've been lucky. Your efforts at mastering the most obscure details of pension policy have been rewarded. You've been asked to be minister for something you know about. Enjoy the day – script some mildly rhetorical but safely anodyne words to say as you go into the department for the first time (but don't be disappointed if the TV cameras are outside the Treasury rather than your department). And then immediately set to work on saying something as interesting as possible as soon as possible.

Reshuffles tend to happen on Thursdays or Fridays; general elections on Thursdays with key ministerial appointments made the next day if the outcome is clear cut. So, if you feel confident enough of the territory, get in early with a Saturday or Sunday political interview. There is likely to be plenty of appetite from the media in getting you in front of the cameras and microphones. But do it only if the following condition is met: you know exactly what the story is going to be. When James Purnell became Secretary of State at DWP, for example, it was clear right from the beginning that he knew what he wanted to do: he wanted to continue with radical reforms to our welfare state. James had been an excellent Pensions Minister when I was at DWP and I knew that he took a keen interest in the wider welfare agenda. David Freud had produced an excellent and hard-hitting report for me on reforming welfare but it had been a struggle to convince Gordon Brown that we should implement his recommendations. After all, these ideas had not originated in the Treasury. The Labour government had devoted a considerable amount of energy to this agenda under Tony Blair. Many of our backbenchers felt we had gone far enough already and wanted a quieter, less demanding programme from the DWP. Welfare reform did not appear to be at the top of Gordon's list of priorities.

James took a different view and decided to reappoint David Freud as his adviser on welfare reform. It was a simple and powerful assertion of the direction he was going to take as the new Secretary of State. James was going to be a reformer and this was the clear message he was sending in reappointing David Freud. No ambiguity or confusing messages here. There was only one problem – the new Prime Minister had a tendency to come out in spots at the mention of David Freud's name. So James also established his own authority and independence of mind from No. 10 – an incredibly bold step indeed.

This episode confirms one other obvious point – but something very easily lost sight of by newly appointed ministers. All new Secretaries of State enjoy a short period of grace after their appointment and get a couple of free wishes. It's very hard to stop a Secretary of State from doing what they want in their first couple of days. The civil servants are keen to impress, even the Permanent Secretary wants to make a good first impression, so the last thing they want to do is say no, even if what you're asking for is the opposite of what they were arguing for until yesterday. And the same is basically true of No. 10: after all, they've just appointed you, so it would be a bit awkward to dismiss your first idea as bonkers. James's decision to reappoint Freud changed the dynamics at Westminster. It was no longer the Tories alone having the courage to implement the tough Freud reforms that the government had abandoned. Instead, the government was now returning to welfare reform, setting its face against Labour rebels. The story was suddenly all about us, the government; we had internalised division. The opposition were written out of the script.

That's the great advantage of government. You can do things. It's only if the government fails to maintain the momentum for reform and change that the opposition gets the chance to fill the vacuum.

Of course, some object that trying to be 'tough' is tokenism. But the hard truth is that in welfare it's only by being tough that you can be soft. It's only by showing that you are prepared to make people take work when it's offered, that you can spend more money on those who genuinely can't find work and need help getting back on their feet again. If you let yourself be put into the 'soft' box on welfare, then it's almost impossible to do anything to tackle disadvantage and unfairness – because it will be more grist to the mill of those who want to caricature you as weak and interested only in spending more taxpayers' money and undermining the work ethic upon which so much depends.

It was an example of a pre-emptive Nixon in China strategy. Because you show people you're prepared to be tough, you get the room for manoeuvre to find money for child poverty, as we did in the next budget with an extra £1.5 billion, or for unemployment, as we did with an extra £5 billion once the credit crunch hit.

So, do that weekend interview. Or make a keynote speech in the first few days after your appointment. You've got a short window of opportunity while the Lobby are interested in the reshuffle. First they want to report who's in and out, up and down. Then they want to say what it means, what's changed, which minister is shaking things up. The truth is it's a race – within a few days, the caravan will have moved on. So, make sure that you are one of the first out of the blocks: you never get a second chance to make that first impression.

And then what? You've made a good start. You've told your department and the public the direction of travel. Now, all you need to do is make it happen. Meantime try to enjoy it; it may not last very long: the average time in any ministerial job is fifteen months, or at least it was before the present government came to power.

And remember: don't be afraid to change things, but don't try to change everything. Above all, stick to that key issue on which you want to make a difference. Because, you know what, if you do you may well succeed.

CHAPTER 2

# I'VE SEEN IT ALL BEFORE

*People with vision usually do more harm than good.*

JOHN MAJOR, 1993

OK, OK; SO YOU'RE HERE to make a difference but can we just have a quick word about that first.

First of all, it's no bad thing. As someone once said, 'democracy is the worst form of government apart from all the others'. Someone has to govern us and all the possible alternatives to elected ministers look a great deal worse to me. You only have to look through a very shortened history of the world to realise that.

And, hard though it may seem to believe, we (that's 'we'

– your civil servants) are not going to be spending all of our time trying to thwart or undermine you. I know that's the great enduring image of *Yes Minister* – and some of the one-liners are still fabulous – but the reality is different.

It's true that we do have some views about what we've seen work in the past and what we've seen fail. And that we have more remaindered copies of Green Papers, White Papers, Papers of indeterminate colour, and some that were published to such a lack of any response whatsoever that even our own press office gave up on trying to interest any journalist in them after the first half hour. But remember that we were complicit in that too. There are people in your department – a bit sad admittedly – who will want nothing better than to call up 'draft White Papers' in their PC memory and crack on with Chapter 1 ('The challenge we face').

So in general you are not going to find some great institutional barrier inside the department – outside may be another matter but we'll come to that later – to doing what you want to do. But that doesn't mean that it's all guaranteed to succeed either. There are going to be plenty of potential pitfalls. It may help, therefore, to tackle a few big questions before your private office starts commissioning hundreds of briefs and documents.

First of all, do you know what you actually want to do?

Sorry if that seems a bit blunt. But most departments have seen more ministers come and go in recent years than they could shake a stick at and some had only the vaguest idea why they'd been appointed and what it was they actually wanted to achieve. If you're truly not in that category, great. Let's hear it from the horse's mouth so we can get going. But if you are please don't feel you have to bluff. It's no crime in our system, and not remotely a rarity either, to end up as the head of a department that you know almost nothing about, feel almost no natural affinity with and rather wish you were somewhere else.

If that is indeed the case why don't you take a bit of time to try and get your thoughts into some sort of order before you make your first big set-piece speech about your vision and aspirations? I know all about getting something into the papers in your first few days before they lose interest and you may need to do that. But then give yourself some space. Tell your private office to keep all but the really unavoidable stuff away from you. Read yourself in to one or two of the big documents your predecessors published – the Executive Summaries will generally do fine; no one other than their authors ever reads the rest anyway; talk to your fellow ministers to see what they think really matters; get a few teach-ins arranged with your civil servants on the issues you think are likely to matter to you most; and go talk to some of the people outside the department who are experts in their fields to hear what they have to say. If you are on speaking terms, then try talking to your immediate predecessor even if – perish the thought – they're now in opposition about where they think they succeeded and where not. More than anything try to listen rather than making great pronouncements; you are going to have more than enough time for those later.

Be wary in that context of the people who tell you that they know exactly what you ought to do. They normally have their own, or somebody else's, axe to grind and they may well have spent years trying to get someone – indeed anyone – to pursue their pet ideas. That applies particularly to the siren voices from No. 10 or No. 11. If the Prime Minister has told you personally what you need to do that's one thing; but be very chary of all the voices who claim to know exactly what the PM or the Chancellor wants. They usually haven't the faintest idea what they are talking about.

More than anything try to get to your own vision of where you think you can really make a difference.

Which brings me to point number two. You can't do everything. Now there are going to be enough times when you think the world is conspiring to force you to do just that and when you're not going to be able to avoid having to mug-up to the eyeballs on stuff in which you have no inherent interest whatsoever, particularly on the days when it all goes pear-shaped. But, if you're really going to stand a chance of making a difference, pick the two or three things (if you're past three take out the red pen and start again) that you absolutely want to achieve and devote yourself relentlessly to them. And make sure that not only your own ministers, but your Permanent Secretary and their top team know that they are your absolute priorities. Don't get distracted, and don't allow others in your department to get distracted either. It will help if you can put all of this in your own words and circulate it to your top team so that your officials really understand what it is you want doing and how you want it done.

And then keep to them. Nothing will destroy your credibility more quickly than telling people your priorities and then changing or dropping them in response to the first bad headline or editorial, the first hint of scepticism from special advisers or No. 10 or the first obstacle along the way. Put them in every speech and every article; it was allegedly Ronald Reagan who said that it's only when you're bored to death of saying it that people are beginning to listen. Repetition is the name of the game. Keep batting away all the other things that the world, and your own department, will want you to adopt as equal priorities to your own two or three. Of course, you'll have to act tactically at times; and there will be days when Harold Macmillan's 'events, dear boy, events' force you to focus exclusively on other things. But, a bit like the self-righting lifeboat, keep coming back with full force to your key priorities just as soon as you are able to.

Thirdly, make sure that No. 10, the Treasury, your Cabinet colleagues – of whom more anon – your Select Committee, and even your driver know that these are your key priorities. Make speeches about them, write articles about them, talk about them in interviews even where the interviews are about something else entirely – 'of course, Jeremy, the truth is that we are not going to make progress on reducing excess sugar consumption unless we tackle the more fundamental issue of welfare dependency' – and hold seminars or conferences about them. None of that, of course, will guarantee that you will achieve them – indeed it could make it all the more embarrassing if you fail to. But it will cause others, particularly inside government, to grasp that these really are your priorities. Even the Treasury is going to think twice about trying to slash the budget of your most prized programme. And No. 10, even if it has bigger fish to fry elsewhere in government, will at least cotton on to how much this matters to you, all of which can only increase your chances of success.

Fourthly, inside the department, try to ensure that you have the best people working on your key priorities. That applies, of course, to your ministerial team and your special advisers. But it applies in spades to your civil servants.

You have to proceed with some caution in this respect.

One of the many checks and balances in the system is that you can't simply go round deciding which civil servants you like the look of and assigning them to new roles. That's down to your department and, ultimately, to your Permanent Secretary. But you can talk to your Permanent Secretary and seek his or her advice on whether the very best people are in the places that matter most to you. Any Permanent Secretary worth their salt is going to want to do that anyway; there is nothing more tedious for a Permanent Secretary than having to listen to endless complaints from ministers about officials who aren't delivering the goods. Once you have a team in place of people you like and trust, pull them inside the tent; don't make them feel that they continually have to appear in front of you as hostile witnesses. Make them feel that they're part of your team – not in a party political sense which would be wholly wrong and make everyone very embarrassed – but simply in terms of wanting them to share your sense of common purpose and enthusiasm.

Fifthly, and importantly, don't assume that you have to build everything afresh from ground zero. It is a barely credible, but nonetheless true, fact that some of what you inherit from your predecessor, even if he or she was your political opponent, and some of what your department is already doing, is probably rather good. It is, of course, terribly tempting, and if there has been a change of government virtually a political necessity, to dismiss everything 'BMOC' (before my own coming) as by definition either irrelevant or simply hopeless; few political careers ever really took off by praising one's predecessors. But the reality is that if you can harness work that is already underway to your own priorities you will gain a huge head start compared with having to start everything afresh.

Sixthly, and also seventhly, eighthly and ninety-firstly, be deeply wary of setting off down the path of reorganising and restructuring your entire department and the institutions that it controls. Now you may have little choice. If it is a cast-iron guarantee in the manifesto on which you've just been elected that you are going to establish a new child protection agency or reorganise the entire NHS yet again you may have simply to do it. And there may genuinely come a point when existing structures really are no longer fit for purpose – our current forty-three police force structure in England and Wales being a good example. But in general re-organisations and restructuring absorb almost infinite amounts of time, money and energy often for little or no benefit, and to the undoubted detriment of your key priorities. You will surprisingly often achieve far more by re-motivating and reinvigorating existing institutions than ever you will by creating new ones.

Finally – and this really is grandmothers and eggs – you're going to need allies. Virtually nothing that you really want to do is going to be neatly self-contained within your own department. You're almost certainly going to need money you don't immediately have; you may well need legislation that is, or is not, in the legislative programme; your plans may well spill over into the responsibilities of colleagues; and it would be amazing if everyone in your own party, let alone the opposition, actually thinks it's a good idea.

As if, in this respect, in telling you all of the above I'm telling you anything much you don't already know. But what is startling is how many ministers know it but ignore it. They think that all of their most cherished ambitions will magically come to pass rather like one of those *Star Trek* episodes where, in the last ten minutes, the aliens self-destruct; the shields that were about to fail suddenly resume operating at full power; Starfleet command sends the relief ship; and Captain Kirk, who appeared to all the world finally to have become a lifeless corpse, resumes triumphant command on the bridge.

Well maybe. But on the Whitehall 'Enterprise' miracles are rare. If you are going to achieve your key priorities it is going to require relentless focus and determination.

CHAPTER 3

# IT CAN BE BETTER

*Politicians are the same everywhere. They promise to build a bridge even when there's no river.*

NIKITA KHRUSHCHEV (1894–1971)

AT THE HEIGHT OF THE credit crunch, a Cabinet minister remarked wistfully that other departments seemed to differ from his in that they usually did what their Secretaries of State had promised the PM they would do. His department did the opposite. For him, the machine was simply broken and no amount of goodwill and effort could get ministers and civil servants working effectively together. In those cases, even if they agree on the direction of travel, there may not be an engine to get the charabanc there.

However, as a keen reader of our advice, and of the first two chapters of our work, you will already have noticed that there is a sweet spot between ministerial exuberance and Permanent Secretary world-weariness. Ministers want to do things but can't do it all themselves – and need someone to warn them if the bus is heading for the cliff. Civil servants hate nothing more than a minister who doesn't know where they want to go and who blames everyone else for their own indecisiveness.

Ask a few older hands for Whitehall's list of best recent ministers – it's likely to include Lawson, Mandelson, Ken Clarke, Milburn, Portillo, Purnell and even Thatcher or Blair. And then ask yourself what they had in common. The answer is pretty clear. They knew what they wanted to do but didn't want to do it all themselves. Some of them even skipped along on the surface of the detail. Many are the ministers who think that success means simply working harder and knowing more than everybody else. And it's certainly true as we note elsewhere that you won't succeed if you're not prepared to work hard. But the risk is that ministers for whom this is their sole strategy frequently run the risk of not spotting the wood for the trees, branches and weeds. The best ministers are forensic when they need to be – in make-or-break Commons debates, in preparing for *Question Time* or media interviews, in presenting to the PM. But they leave themselves with enough time and space to do what only they can do – set direction, make decisions, open up new territory, foresee danger.

The sweet spot is a minister setting the direction and the civil service helping them to get there. Like much else this is easier said than done. But there are some basic ground rules to help you.

First, get the balance right between priority and routine. We both agree that a Secretary of State has to set a direction, that you can't have a hatful of priorities, and that probably only one or two issues are going to define your (possibly brief) time at the helm. You need to combine that with a method to deal with everything that falls outside of your top priorities – and there will be an awful lot of that. The obvious approach is to delegate many if not most of these more routine issues to your team of junior ministers to deal with. This will not only let you focus on the issues you have decided to prioritise, it will also empower your junior ministers to be effective within the department. Civil servants will know that they have authority to make decisions and that you trust them to do this on your behalf.

Of course it's important to strike the right balance between delegation and oversight. Ask your Permanent Secretary to do you a monthly note on all the main areas in the department, and to warn you quickly if there's a serious emerging problem. Get your junior ministers to talk about their areas of responsibility at your weekly stocktakes (and try not to cancel them too frequently). Try and involve all of your ministerial team in the overall work of the department and don't allow them to retreat into their own portfolios.

Second, rely on your civil servants but don't depend exclusively on them. There are some parts of the job that only they can do – run your private office, manage the policy process, commission services. There are other parts where they are often the best placed – devising policy, paying benefits, writing legislation. But note the use of the word 'often'. There will undoubtedly be times when it will be sensible for you to access a range of views – either in collaboration with each other or sometimes in competition. If you ever make it as far as Part II of our book on some of the lessons we have learned you'll see that we argue for an opening up of the policy process not only to improve the quality of policy advice in the short term but also to build the capability of Whitehall, through competition and collaboration. You may or may not agree with that but at the very least you need to reduce the risk of 'group think' – a real occupational hazard in Whitehall – and make sure you are getting access to the best ideas and the latest research. Don't assume that this will automatically be the case.

Third, think hard about how involved you want to be in operational delivery. You may, of course, be in a department like Culture, Media and Sport, or Energy and Climate Change, which operates almost exclusively through others and which has little direct executive authority. But if, by contrast, you're heading a department like DWP or the Ministry of Justice which directly runs big direct delivery bodies like Jobcentre Plus or the Prison Service you need to decide what role you want to play. You can't just ignore the delivery side and hope for the best; on the day that some ghastly delivery failure occurs it's going to be you at the despatch box trying to explain what's happened and taking the rap for it. On the other hand, trying to micro-manage the business of organisations the size of a FTSE 100 company is simply going to be impossible even if you have the requisite skills – which you almost certainly don't. So you need to agree a set of ground rules with your Permanent Secretary which cover what you expect to be told and how frequently, the level of involvement that you do want to have and, crucially, how you will both operate on the occasions – which will surely come – when things do go wrong. The key is likely to be mutual trust and support. But that has to be worked at; it won't just happen.

Fourth, never forget you're a politician not an administrator.

You are there to sort out and manage the politics associated with your ministerial portfolio, a basic fact which quite a lot of Cabinet ministers somehow seem to forget. More of this later, but a good rule of thumb is that relationships precede action. If you get on with a Cabinet colleague, they're much more likely to agree with your proposed policy, unless it's totally barking. And if it is, they'll be much more likely to tell you privately (rather than in front of everyone else) to try to save you from yourself. These relationships don't make themselves. They need effort, time and space. In opposition it was easy to arrange to sit down with your shadow Cabinet colleagues. In government this will be harder than you think. For Whitehall, that means accepting that you will sometimes have meetings with colleagues without minutes – indeed without private secretaries. A dinner in the Commons or a coffee to shoot the breeze can save weeks of Whitehall correspondence.

Finally – and this is just a taster, we devote a whole chapter to it later on – put time into the relationship with your Permanent Secretary. You don't have to like them (though it helps if you do) but you do need to work out how to work with them. Meet them regularly; every Monday morning can be good, unless you're like a bear with a sore head at the start of the week in which case find a better time. Try not to have any secrets. Never embarrass them in front of their juniors. They've got to the top of the Whitehall tree and deserve the same respect you yourself probably expect from others. And believe it or not, they are there to help. They can help and mostly they want to. But they can also stop and block. Make clear that you do want to be told – privately – if they think you are making a major mistake or acting in any way improperly. Make clear what your absolute priorities are and ask for their support to help you achieve them. Make clear also your own expectations of them, not least that you want no surprises. But above all, make clear that you want them on your side. Other than your partner and the Prime Minister, they are probably going to be the most important person in your life for the next few years.

Of course you can do all this and still fail. Indeed that applies to all the advice that we are sufficiently presumptuous to offer in the whole of this book. But, like much else, politics is about percentages. You can never reduce the risks of failure to zero but you can move the odds in your favour.

CHAPTER 4

# ANALYSIS AND EXPERTS

*An expert is a man who has made all the mistakes which can be made in a very narrow field.*

NIELS HENRIK BOHR (1885–1962)

SO WE'RE AGREED; YOU WANT to make a difference; you've met your Permanent Secretary and some of your civil servants and you've thought through what you really want to achieve. But are you confident you know enough about the portfolio you've ended up with or about the key policy areas you want to tackle?

Now it may be that the answer to both is 'yes'. This may be one of those rare occasions – and when they do happen it's not always by pure chance – where a minister is appointed to a role which they really do know about, either because they have shadowed it in opposition for a long time or because it is genuinely their own field of expertise. Even then the case for having some other sources of expertise available to you is compelling, not least to avoid the risk of thinking you have to know, still less do, it all yourself.

But if the position is the much more usual one that you are not remotely expert yourself in the area for which you now find yourself responsible, you need to think where and how you are going to acquire the analysis and expertise you need. Of course your junior ministers may well be able to help, particularly if one or more of them actually has some expertise in your department's business. Your special advisers, too, of whom much more anon, are going to have an important role to play, although they are likely to be so bound up with helping you avoid the political pitfalls that they may or may not be able to bring anything serious to the party in terms of real subject matter knowledge.

Against that background the first question to ask is the extent to which your civil servants have the expertise you need. There's much more about your civil servants, and how you might want to work with them, later in this book. But for now the question is a narrower one; how expert and knowledgeable are they really about the business of your department?

Your Permanent Secretary is inevitably going to find this a somewhat uncomfortable question to answer. He or, much more commonly than in the past, she is going to be pretty reluctant to admit that their department doesn't pass muster in that respect. Which is why it's probably better to pose the question somewhat differently by asking which, in their view, are the department's areas of greatest strength in terms of expertise and analysis and which, by contrast, are relatively weaker. Even the foremost exponents of the 'Sir Humphrey' school of obfuscation are going to find that a difficult question to evade altogether. Most Permanent Secretaries, who do not come remotely from that school, will try and give you a reasonably honest answer.

The truth is that most government departments do have considerable knowledge and expertise within their civil service ranks – much more than you might instinctively believe. There are likely to be some genuine experts both buried away in the system and amongst your senior advisers. But there will also be lots of people who, rather like ministers, have moved pretty rapidly from job to job, generally not staying in any one long enough to become truly expert in any one subject. They will often be very skilful in the business of government and know a good deal about process, but they won't necessarily be any more knowledgeable than you about the underlying subject matter.

How to find out who's who in this respect is not always easy. The civil service has become far less hierarchical and grade conscious in recent years but, compared to most outside organisations, it is still much more based around seniority than you are likely to have experienced, particularly in the private sector. It is one of the few organisations where people are every bit as likely to introduce themselves to you by telling you their grade and title – 'I'm the deputy director for procurement policy' – as they are by telling you who they are and what they do – 'I'm John Smith from the Procurement team'. One consequence of this is that, particularly in your early days, it's likely to be one of the senior civil servants who will lead off on whatever subject you are discussing – with other people staying pretty silent round the table. That can make it quite tough to work out who really knows about the subject you want to talk about.

There is no miracle answer to this but there are some pointers. Perhaps the most important is to consciously let conversation flow round your table. Go out of your way to seek opinions and don't tell people instantly what the answer is even if you're pretty sure you know. Even more important, don't bite people's heads off for saying something you don't agree with, and don't tell them that a child of three could have come up with a more convincing answer than the one they've just given, even if that's what you think. If you do then most of the civil servants you see, particularly the more junior ones, are going to play for safety, only speaking when they feel they have to for fear of getting publicly done over yet again. By contrast if you let discussion range, and make clear you want it to, you will gradually find not only that people will begin to tell you what they really think but also that you will begin, quite quickly, to get a sense of who amongst your civil servants has the most to offer. It will also in general be a much more enjoyable way of doing business. And let your Permanent Secretary and your private office know that, while you don't want regular meetings that would fill the Albert Hall, you are keen to hear from people – however junior they may be in the hierarchy – who have the knowledge to help you get to the right answer.

There have to be some limits, of course. On the days on which the proverbial has just hit the fan or when you simply have no time for discussion and debate, you will need to be more direct. And don't go so far in pursuit of a gradeless approach that you forget who the senior people in the room are altogether. They won't thank you if you appear to undervalue their opinions in the presence of their own staff and, despite what popular mythology might suggest, they tend to have got to the top because they are good, often very good. But in general the more open to ideas and debate you are, the more you will not only get better ideas and proposals but also a better idea of who really knows what they are talking about. They are the people you can then make sure, through your private office, that you see the most of.

The issue of what to do if you come to the conclusion that some parts of your department simply don't have the knowledge or expertise you need is trickier. One option is, of course, to discuss with your Permanent Secretary the options for strengthening the team or teams you have most concern about. That is certainly worth doing; while it is theoretically the case that civil service staffing is the Permanent Secretary's responsibility, not yours, as we've already said, the Permanent Secretary is going to have a strong self-interest in trying to meet your concerns – put at its simplest they don't want this to be the sole subject of conversation every time they walk into your room – and they may well be able to switch people around to try and give you one or more people in whom you have greater confidence. So if you are unhappy with a particular team or even individual, say so – though do so privately and quietly to the Permanent Secretary, rather than publicly or noisily.

You may well conclude, however, that this simply isn't enough and that you need access to a wider range of advice and expertise than your civil servants alone can give you. Indeed you may very well reach that conclusion even if you think you are being well served by your civil servants but simply want access to a wider range of opinions and views. In that case you have a number of options available to you which are not necessarily mutually exclusive.

The first is clearly to bring one or more people in. That has become much more commonplace in recent years and, although you may still find some institutional resistance to the idea, there is no doubt that you can do it. You need, of course, to know who it is you want to bring in and have some idea what you want them to do. You also need to think about the level at which you want them to operate. There can be real advantage in getting a senior and widely respected outsider to join the team, particularly if you know and have confidence in them. But in general – see our advice on 'Goats' ('a government of all the talents') in our later chapter – the more senior the level the more fraught this can become, with the clear risk that the person concerned ends up jockeying for power with your junior ministers or senior civil servants. What often works better – and is almost always easier to arrange – is to bring in one or at most a couple of people to support you closer to the engine room than the bridge. The aim is to give you and your civil servants access to a degree of specialism and expertise that you either don't have or at least would like more of.

Where are such people likely to come from? Plainly that will depend on the subject matter – if you want an expert on nuclear fission then the sources are likely to be more limited than if you want help with pensions reform – but there are some obvious places to look. One is clearly a think tank or research institute in your chosen field; another a university or other academic institution; a third could be a management consultancy or private sector company (though you need to be very careful to avoid anything that could be seen as a conflict of interest – appointing someone from an arms manufacturer to help you reshape defence policy is never going to be your best ever idea). Probably more important than the source is the type of person they are. While the first criteria has to be that they can bring you the expertise you want, they also need to be able to cope with working inside a big machine and will also need, therefore, at least a modicum of diplomatic and interpersonal skills. Neither the Rottweiler nor the mad professor is likely to be the personality profile you most want.

Having identified the person or persons you want you need then to talk to your Permanent Secretary before doing anything else. That is not just because they or the department may know something about the person in question that you don't ('I'm not absolutely sure we want to bring a convicted fraudster into the department, Minister') but because they are more likely than you to be able to come up with a way of getting them on board which won't lead to the outbreak of World War Three. Moreover, trying to bring someone in over your Permanent Secretary's dead body is never a particularly clever thing to do. You may succeed but you are likely to discover only later at what cost; far better to enlist their support in getting the deed done.

If all of that can be worked through, the final thing you need to do before Mr or Mrs X walks through the door is agree between the two of you explicitly how you want them to work. In particular you need to make clear that their role is to help you succeed and not to maraud through your department like some latter-day Barbary Coast pirate. Make explicit that, while they are there to give you their unfettered advice, you want them to work as far as possible with your junior ministers and your civil servants and not against them. Doing this doesn't guarantee that their appointment won't end in tears but it will make the chances a good deal better.

You may, of course, decide that bringing someone in is not the right course or not sufficient. In that case the next option to think about may be commissioning someone or some organisation out there to do one or more pieces of work for you.

The first question in this respect is whether you want a one-off piece of work or whether you want the continuing availability of an external organisation. That matters not least because the procurement rules that you have to follow are different in the two cases. If essentially you want an outside expert to produce a report for you on a single issue – such as whether to cull badgers if serendipity has taken you to Defra – then, so long as you can identify a sane and rational person with the necessary credibility who is willing to take this on, it is relatively easy to arrange. Your Permanent Secretary is unlikely to think that they have to go through a competitive procurement process and, so long as the person isn't your brother-in-law or a major donor to the party, there shouldn't be any great difficulty in getting them on board.

There can be real advantages in going down this route. If you genuinely don't know what to do about a particular issue, or you think you know where you want to get to but are much less clear as to how to get there, a report from a respected outsider may well help. Moreover it has the added advantage that if they come up with something totally barking – let's breed lots more badgers and have them adopted as pets by local schools – you can simply shelve their report as 'requiring further and detailed consideration'. And even if you do think you know what needs to be done there are times when having that endorsed by a respected outside expert can be worth its weight in gold in terms of getting the policy accepted in the House and more widely.

The alternative of getting an external organisation on board to be able to advise you over a longer timescale is more difficult. That will inevitably mean going for a competitive procurement which will take time and money. But even more importantly it means that you can't be sure of the outcome. So if your aim is to get a particular organisation alongside you, perhaps because you've worked with them before or simply because they are highly respected in their field, you have to face the risk that they may not win the competition, not least because it's your department's procurement people who are going to run the competition and decide the outcome without reference to you (that may seem somewhat odd given that it's meant to be your department but only suicidally inclined ministers are likely to want to involve themselves personally in deciding the result of individual procurement exercises). You can try to reduce the risks of getting the 'wrong' result by agreeing a specification for the tender which makes it more likely that your preferred organisation will make a strong showing, but it's a pretty risky route if, as surely you do, you want to be seen as whiter than white.

Of course none of this matters if you genuinely are open-minded as to who wins. In that case you can afford to be much more relaxed about the outcome and concentrate on what it is you are trying to get from such an arrangement. The potential benefit is in giving you an alternative source of ongoing advice which you can turn to alongside, or as an alternative to, the advice of your civil servants. That may be genuinely valuable especially if you think that your department is simply in a mind-set that you don't agree with or are at least sceptical about. And, more generally, as we set out in Part II of the book, there are good arguments as to why we think it would be inherently healthier if there was much less of a Whitehall monopoly over the policy process. On the other hand, leaving aside cost (and arrangements of this kind are unlikely to come cheap), bringing in an external organisation will be seen as much more of a challenge to your own civil servants and the potential risk is that you end up with a tiger by the tail and come to regret the day you ever invited them into your department. So this is not something to be embarked upon lightly, but don't be put off if you are convinced that it is the right thing to do.

Of course as well as considering all of the options set out above you need to go on doing the simple things like continuing to read what people are writing about your department and its policies – though you will rapidly find just how little time you have for that – and going out of your way to meet people who you think have something to offer. Above all, keep looking outwards and don't allow yourself to get completely sucked in to your department's business and nothing else. Tell your office that you want time set aside each week to go and see something or talk to someone at first hand. Ask to meet with groups of the junior civil servants in the department who actually have to deliver your policies day by day but who you may almost never otherwise meet. Invite in some of the more respected academics in your department's field to hear their views on what you should be doing. All of that will not only help you do the job better; it will also keep you saner for the day when you resume normal life.

CHAPTER 5

# THE SECRETARY OF STATE

*It has been the great fault of our politicians that they have all wanted to do something.*

ANTHONY TROLLOPE (1815–1882)

WE COVER LATER IN THIS volume some of the more philosophical demands of ministerial office and how you might approach them (see 'Ministers'). We thought that in this short chapter we might get rather more into the nitty-gritty of your day-to-day life now that you are the Secretary of State (congratulations again by the way on landing the job) and that you might value a quick A-Z guide to some of the practicalities. It's a bit hit and miss and you probably know most of it already but you may just want to dip in and out occasionally for reference. So here goes.

## A – ACTING

IF I'D WANTED to act I would have gone to RADA, I hear you say. Too true, but equally true that quite a lot of the time you are nevertheless going to have to be the actor on the stage. That does not mean making it up as you go along, still less being economical with the truth (contrary to popular opinion we've met very few ministers who wanted to do either). But it does mean that on most days for as long as you are Secretary of State you are going to have to go from one meeting or engagement to another often at bewildering pace. That's not easy even on the good days; on the bad ones, where almost everything you touch seems to have turned to dust, it can seem simply overwhelming. It's on those days though as you walk out of your office to give the speech, meet the interest group or attend yet another numb-skullingly tedious Cabinet Committee on a subject in which you have virtually no interest that you have to become the actor – confident, good-humoured, attentive and articulate – no matter how fed up you are actually feeling. Not easy but absolutely necessary to your political survival. So start practising.

## B – BOXES

THE FIRST MINISTERIAL red box you ever got – as one of us recalls in our later chapter on private office – seemed unbelievably exciting; by contrast as Secretary of State the box or boxes that your office will give or send you virtually every single night will come to seem the ultimate drudgery – full of long, dreary or just plain incomprehensible submissions. Now there are things you can do about this, like setting clear rules on the number of boxes you will take, when you will take them and how you expect work to be presented – though be prepared for your private office to ignore the rules when it suits them. And your private office will be able to help, if you want them to, by prioritising, summarising and highlighting what they think you most need to see. In the end, however, there is no substitute for simply doing the work. You need to work out a pattern for when you are going to do your box and then stick to it in all but the most exceptional of circumstances. You will in the end feel a lot better as a result.

## C – CABINET COMMITTEES

SAVE FOR RARE days of real drama – to go to war or not, threatened resignations or the completely unexpected – Cabinet itself is generally a piece of stage management used for the most part to tell colleagues more widely of decisions that have already been taken. How much of the real decision-taking gets taken formally at all – as opposed to round the Prime Minister's famous sofa – depends to a large extent on the style of the Prime Minister of the day. But there is no doubt that more of the real work, and more of the real decisions, get taken in Cabinet Committees than in Cabinet itself. Which committees you are on, and which you actually attend, is not wholly in your hands – the former in particular will generally be decided by No. 10 and the Cabinet Office. But for those committees your department is invited to be a member of you need to decide which you will attend personally and which you will delegate to other members of your ministerial team. And, having done so, you need to ensure that they, and you, are properly briefed and prepared before you walk through the committee door. Nothing will undermine you and your department more than to be seen as unprepared and unpersuasive. And decisions that go the wrong way for you and the department will be incredibly hard to unpick afterwards.

## D – DEVOLUTION

BY THE TIME you are reading this the result of the independence referendum in Scotland may have changed forever the nature of the UK. Or not. But whatever the outcome you need to understand, and think hard about, the devolution dimension of almost everything you do. Even if your department's writ runs essentially only in England – Education for example – or only in England and Wales, you still need to be alive to the potential pitfalls in terms of what you want to do by comparison with what is happening in the rest of the UK. If you are in a department whose writ still runs in other countries within the UK – such as DWP or Defence – you need to be perpetually sensitive to the devolved dimension and how your department's actions will be perceived away from the Westminster prism. You may well want to think about setting up some piece of machinery inside your department – if it doesn't already exist – to watch this for you. That should reduce the risks of getting it wrong simply by accident.

## E – EUROPE

YOU WILL HAVE your own views on Europe and whether you see it as the ultimate betrayal of Westminster sovereignty, the finest example of international co-operation since World War Two or, more likely, somewhere between the two. And there is, in any event, a separate chapter on Europe elsewhere in our book for those readers who get that far. But love it or loathe it politically, it is highly unlikely that you can avoid the importance of Europe for your department. There are few parts of Whitehall now into which EU legislation does not reach and some where at least as much is decided in Brussels as in London. So you need to decide how much of your time you are going to give to EU business personally and, if you do not want to be perpetually on the Eurostar – no one flies to Brussels any more – how you want your other ministers involved. And that involves not just attendance at formal councils and other meetings but also the bilateral contacts you almost certainly need to have with your opposite numbers in other member states and with the European Commission. Very little of this is glamorous and much of it tedious. But its importance to your ability to deliver your agenda is, for better or worse, likely to be substantial.

## F – FRIENDS

A STRANGE ONE this. Surely your friends are your own business and nothing to do with your role as Secretary of State. True, but only up to a point. It's not just that now you are the Secretary of State you'll discover that you have far more friends than ever you knew you had. It's also that some of them are likely to ask for your time, your support or even your patronage. The obvious advice – but not so obvious as to be not worth saying – is to be extraordinarily cautious. Don't forget all those ministers – there could even be some amongst the pictures of your predecessors hanging outside your office

– who were brought down by seemingly innocuous favours to friends or partners or by blurring the boundaries between the private and official sides of their lives. The simple maxim is 'if in doubt don't'. And even if you are not in doubt it may well be sensible to seek the advice of your Permanent Secretary before doing anything, however apparently innocent, that could conceivably be seen as improper or questionable.

## G – GOVERNANCE

THIS SEEMS DEADLY dull – shall we go on to 'H'? But actually it's about how your department is run and whether it is run well or badly. It is no accident that governance now occupies so much time in private sector boardrooms and amongst their non-executives. Put at its simplest you and your Permanent Secretary have to know how the department is run, who in practice is in charge of what and how you are going to split the responsibilities between you. A key issue is agreeing how you want to run the departmental board, which you are likely to chair, who you want on it and what it should discuss and decide. It also involves deciding the relationship you want to have with the department's lead and other non-executive directors. There is no magic blueprint for any of this and different structures are likely to be required for different departments. The only certainty is that if you ignore all of this completely you are likely to end up paying the price.

## H – HOLIDAYS

SOUNDS MORE FUN than 'governance'. And it is. The first rule is that you absolutely need during the year to take some genuine holiday. You deserve it and so do your family or those closest to you; probably even more than you. The second rule is that when you are on holiday it needs to be real. That means not ringing your private office and your Spads (special advisers) three times a day. It means not spending hours every day reading and responding to your e-mails. And it means not listening obsessively to every news bulletin or watching Sky or BBC World for hours every day on the hotel TV. Of course, depending on your actual role, there can be truly exceptional circumstances which may mean your having to spend hours on the phone or even, in extremis, having to cut short your holiday and return. But you'll know pretty quickly if it's something of that magnitude. For the rest turn off the mobile and pour yourself another glass of wine. At the same time make sure your Private Secretary knows where you are and how to contact you (maybe your partner can leave their mobile on) and then trust them to bother you only if absolutely necessary. Amazingly the world will still be there when you get back (indeed your junior ministers may even enjoy their moment in the metaphorical sun while you're enjoying the real thing. Oh, and don't worry about them upstaging you – it's only August!).

## I – INVITATIONS

YOU ARE GOING to get loads. Everyone who is anyone is going to want you to speak at their conference, open their event and visit their programme. They will approach you formally by letter and e-mail, via your Spads and private office, through your constituency and face to face if they think they can get hold of you. Of course some of these invitations you will have to take up; it's hard for the Home Secretary to turn down the Police Federation Annual Conference or the Education Secretary the NUT. And some you will absolutely want to do. But you need to be pretty selective if you are not going to be run ragged; and to have a system which allows you to decide what you want to do rather than allowing other people to decide that for you. Try at all costs too to avoid getting bounced by the personal approach. Plead the need to consult the diary and know a bit more about it. Ask them to write in. And above all, make sure you get yourself a truly first-rate Diary Manager in your private office who can courteously hold even the great and the good at bay while you decide what you want to do – and what you don't. Indeed you may want to go further and set some key ground rules with them for keeping the diary under control such as setting fixed times for visits, keeping chunks of the day free and so on.

## J – JUNIOR MINISTERS

TRICKY. YOU WERE one. And the chances are you felt deeply frustrated at times at being excluded from much of the key decision-making while being asked to take on everything under the sun that your then Secretary of State could not be bothered to do themselves or felt was just too much like hard work. You swore that if you ever made it to Secretary of State you were going to act differently. The only trouble is that now you have you are not quite so sure. Pushing loads of tedious stuff on to your junior ministers is beginning to seem quite attractive. Now there is no simple answer to this one. But there is probably quite a good rule of thumb. If you can get your junior ministers to feel that they are, with you, part of a genuine team, you are likely to get far more genuine support and buy-in from them than if they feel that they are simply glorified dogsbodies. That means involving them before key decisions are made, asking for their views and listening to what they say, and giving them real decision-making authority over large swathes of the department's business without having to seek your authority. But it also requires setting some clear ground rules about when you do expect to be consulted and about the behaviours that you do and do not expect to see, including within the department. Getting this right requires effort, patience and leadership. But the payback if you can get it right will be substantial.

## K – KNITTING

NOT LITERALLY – though there's nothing wrong with it if it grabs you. But metaphorically, now that you're a Cabinet minister, you need to decide how much of your time and effort you are going to give to government-wide issues and how much to spend on your own department's business. There's no right answer to this; much will turn on your own inclination, your position within the party and what others ask you to do. But there's probably a word of caution; very few people succeed at Cabinet level by neglecting their own department. If you are not seen to be on top of its agenda and very clearly in charge of its direction you are likely to find yourself in trouble pretty quickly. So sticking to your knitting – at least in your early days as Secretary of State – has a lot to be said for it.

## L – LAWYERS

NOW THAT YOU'RE the Secretary of State you're likely to be surprised at the number of times that you are told that something you want to do is legally dubious or outside of your powers. And you may be surprised also at the number of legal challenges that are brought against you and your department. That, of course, is why your department has lawyers, but practice varies quite widely in Whitehall as to how much direct contact they have with ministers. One tip, on issues that really matter, is to ask to see your lawyers' advice in full rather than having it summarised by policy officials and, if you are still unclear or worried, to ask to see the most senior lawyers concerned face to face so you can hear their views direct and ask questions. That will help you decide whether your department is using supposed legal advice as a way of blocking ministerial decisions they don't like. It will also give you a sense of which of your senior lawyers are the ones who simply tell you what you can't do and which are the ones who will help you find solutions. Where an issue is of really key importance, and particularly if your legal advice is less than clear, you can, of course, ask for it to be referred to the government's Law Officers for an opinion. But don't do that lightly; once the Law Officers have pronounced you are pretty well committed to following their advice. So go down that route only if you're certain you want to know the answer.

## M – MONEY

BY DEFINITION THERE'S never enough. And that applies whether you're the ultimate big spender or a former Chief Secretary who led the war on waste – it's odd how perspectives change as you exit the Treasury (if you've never been in the Treasury there's more about it later in the book). That means that much of your time is going to be spent trying to chisel out some of your department's existing spending to fund your new programme or initiative. That is never easy. Your officials will, at the drop of a hat, paint you lurid pictures of the likely consequences of cutting any existing budget on which your attention alights. This is one area where you almost certainly do need the help of your Permanent Secretary. He or she is likely to have a much better idea than you can ever hope to have on where there is scope for cutting existing programmes without it leading to total mayhem. And he or she can almost certainly bang heads together with you not in the room much more effectively than you can do so with him or her in it. None of this means that the money can always be found. It may just be too big a sum and you're going to be in obvious trouble if the Permanent Secretary thinks it lousy value for money. But this is one area where working with your Permanent Secretary is likely to pay many more dividends than working against them.

## N – NEVER SAY NEVER

OR ONLY VERY rarely. There will, of course, be some issues on which your personal position, or that of your party, is so absolute as to brook no room for doubt. But for the rest, events have a terrible habit of making your cast-iron pronouncements of last year or even last month look unsustainable. Now this is quite difficult territory. Neither your supporters nor the public are likely to warm to a minister who appears unable to utter any sentence without at least three qualifying sub-clauses (your civil servants are quite good enough at that in any event). On the other hand, having to eat your own words is never the most delectable of courses. So it does generally make sense to leave yourself some wriggle room to cater for the unexpected, particularly where the future is unpredictable. And you can always present it as a virtue in contrast to your opponents who are, of course, blinded to reality and stuck in the past.

## O – OMBUDSMEN

A STRANGELY NON-PC title. Have you ever heard anyone refer to an Ombudswoman? And they come in different forms; the Parliamentary and Health Service Ombudsman, the Pensions Ombudsman, the Local Government Ombudsman and many more including, somewhat bizarrely, a Removals Industry Ombudsman who you could no doubt complain to on the day your red box turns up in Washington rather than Warrington. A Google search suggests that there are some 9 million references to ombudsmen to be found although, thankfully, somewhat fewer actual post holders. But, depending on the department you are heading, they can be both important and influential, particularly where they are dealing with complaints against your department from multiple parties – class actions in effect – rather than simply from dissatisfied individuals. Their direct day-to-day contact with the department will be almost entirely with your civil servants – up to and including the Permanent Secretary in the most significant cases – but it's still worth having them on your radar screen and perhaps meeting the key Ombudsman (or even woman) from time to time. You probably want at least to be forewarned if they are about to release a damning and potentially expensive condemnation of the department's actions.

## P – PRIME MINISTER

THAT'S ONE THING you are unlikely to need any advice on. You know who's in charge and what they expect (though see our later chapter on No. 10 more generally). But it is perhaps worth a word about all those at No. 10 who perpetually claim to be acting on the Prime Minister's instructions or, at the very least, to know exactly what he or she wants. Now sometimes they do. If you or your office get a call from the PM's Principal Private Secretary relaying the PM's views you can be 99 per cent certain that you are getting it straight from the horse's mouth. But there are lots of other people much lower down the food chain at No. 10 who nevertheless still have access to the notepaper. When they tell you or your department that the PM wants this, that or the other they may or may not have any genuine Prime Ministerial authority for saying so. Just as likely is that they have a view, or a pet project that they want to get off the ground, and that this is the best way of trying to get it to happen. The moral here, particularly if what No. 10 is asking for seems particularly daft, is not to allow your office or your department to see everything emanating from No. 10 as holy writ. If it makes sense and is affordable you may well want to do it. But if not push back. You will be surprised when you do at how often the idea simply disappears.

## Q – QUIDDITCH

THIS IS A test really of how well you know your *Harry Potter*. It's the game where the teams have to keep all the balls in the air and not let the outliers escape. Now you may be beginning to see the relevance. This is the life of a Secretary of State to a 't'. You are following our advice and concentrating on the two or three things that you believe really matter when suddenly you are laid low by the one you never saw coming. By definition there's no answer to this. It's just life and sometimes you're just going to have to deal with it. But you can reduce the chances of being 'blown off course' – as it was once famously put – by encouraging a culture of genuine openness and approachability amongst your junior ministers and your civil servants. If people think it's safe to tell you things without getting their heads blown off they are much more likely to tell you about the potential minefield before the mines start exploding.

## R – REGULATORS

CHANCES ARE THAT your department will have dealings with at least one regulator, if not more. This is quite difficult territory. Regulators are normally set up under statute to have a high degree of autonomy; indeed if your department sponsors one or more it will be your duty to support and defend that independence. At the same time the decisions that regulators reach can have substantial impact on the work of your department and, indeed, on what you yourself want to achieve. You need to be very careful here not to be seen to be trying to influence your regulator or regulators improperly. On the other hand, you do need them to understand what you are about and how you see the issues. That suggests meeting the relevant regulators reasonably frequently and encouraging your department, and indeed your Permanent Secretary, to stay close to them. You will also want to ensure that they feel that your department is being open and forthcoming in its dealings with them. In the end the better informed they are the more sensible they are likely to be in their decisions.

## S – SELECT COMMITTEES

YOU CERTAINLY DON'T need telling about the importance of Select Committees in general and your own departmental Select Committee in particular. Increasingly they provide what the Chamber of the House of Commons often does not; i.e. rational discussion of your department's policies and programmes and sensible enquiry into your proposed plans. Therein, of course, lies the risk. It's easy enough to shrug off the opposition's attacks on you and your policies in the House as motivated by a mixture of spite and ignorance; far harder to do so in response to an agreed all-party report from your own departmental Select Committee tearing your proposed policy to shreds. Now you will have your own coping strategy for this; and much will turn on the personalities involved, particularly the chair, and your own relationships with them. But there are some simple dos and don'ts that probably help. Do give your Select Committee lots of your and your department's time. They will be better informed as a result and feel, if nothing else, that they are at least being taken seriously. Be prepared to hold informal sessions with them so they can feel they are really influencing policy and take really seriously what the chair says to you, particularly in private. Don't dismiss the recommendations in their reports lightly. There will inevitably be voices in the department saying that they have simply got the wrong end of the stick and wanting you to say so. But they may not have and it may in any event cost you relatively little to say 'yes' rather than 'no'. More than anything prepare really thoroughly for your own appearances in front of the committee. Not only will you do better than if you attempt to bluff your way through but it will again indicate the respect you are giving them. It can only help.

## T – TRAVEL

THERE WILL COME a point at which you will want to go somewhere other than to your constituency, the House or the Sewage Manufacturers Association annual dinner; in other words abroad. That can seem very enticing particularly if it's wet and cold at home or you're just fed up with the daily Westminster grind. And there is no reason why you shouldn't. It would be astonishing if there was nothing to be learned from what other countries are doing in your department's field. But you do need to tread, and travel, cautiously. More than ever ministers are vulnerable to being accused of junketing at the taxpayer's expense. So think carefully about where you want to go – it may not necessarily have to be Australia, New Zealand or California; take advice not least from the Foreign Office on who you should meet and what you should see; keep the numbers on the trip with you down to those you really need – it's not a reward for hard work; and leave your partner at home. Make sure, too, that you follow your department's travel policy in relation to class of travel and hotel accommodation. If in doubt consult your Permanent Secretary and get their blessing. It may all make for a somewhat less grand trip. But it will keep you from being in the headlines for all the wrong reasons.

## U – USUAL SUSPECTS

INEVITABLY THERE ARE going to be lots of people and organisations with whom you and your department can't avoid dealing even if you wanted to. And, on the upside, many of them have lots to offer. But all organisations, and Whitehall departments are no exception, can all too easily become trapped into only consulting and meeting with those they already know. So it is worth thinking quite hard about whether you want to break the mould and, if so, how you should go about it. It will almost certainly be harder work, and there will be more risks, in consulting with, for example, community groups, local leaders and the like, but the potential benefits are large if it helps you get a broader perspective. And there are lots of interesting techniques around now – such as deliberative polling – for consulting with the public other than via the classic mediums of consultation documents, which ordinary members of the public never read, or opinion polls with all their limitations. Going down these routes will also make your department seem more open to ideas and diversity; no bad thing in a world where people see government as ever more distant from them.

## V – VERSION CONTROL

THIS REALLY IS a nuts and bolts one, but you may still remember the department which contrived to send out the version of the Secretary of State's letter with all the track changes and commentary still showing ('I've removed the words "as you will appreciate" as he barely appreciates anything these days') which still causes the relevant minister and officials to break out in a cold sweat to this day. So in an era in which documents can go through any number of drafts on their way to you, and then more while you and your Spads change them further, ask your Principal Private Secretary to come up with the most foolproof way known to mankind to make sure that what goes out in your name really is the version you have finally approved.

## W – WALL-TO-WALL

THIS IS HOW, if you let them, your private office will organise every working day that you are in the office. You shouldn't blame them too much; they in turn are under huge pressure from your junior ministers, from every part of your department – including from senior officials who will have far more influence over their future careers than you will – and from any number of external bodies all of whom are saying that if they don't get to talk to the Secretary of State in the next forty-eight hours the end of the world will surely follow. Small wonder that there are no gaps between nine in the morning ('I wonder if we can just squeeze that one in at 8.30?') and when they wearily wave you off to the House or your evening engagement at seven in the evening offering to carry your three red boxes down to the car with you. Some of this just goes with the territory; if you really want a life say no when the PM next offers you a job. But it doesn't mean that you are powerless to do anything about it. As already noted, the key, with your Diary Secretary and your Principal Private Secretary, is to wrest back control of your diary and steadfastly refuse to allow anything to go in it without your agreement. You will have to be brutal to succeed. But you will be amazed at how many of those world-ending issues somehow get resolved without your intervention. And you may get just a little of your life back.

## X – XMAS

A BIT LIKE 'Holidays' (see 'H' above) – make sure you stop for it; buy all of your office presents and take them out for lunch – they've worked incredibly hard all year; find time to buy some really nice things for your nearest and dearest – they've put up with you all year; and then overdo the turkey and mince pies without a red box in sight; you deserve it too.

## Y – YESTERDAY

DON'T BROOD ON it even if it was the day from hell. You are going to have some really gruesome days, as our later chapters describe, sometimes of your own making but just as likely not. Learn the lessons, of course, and if you have made a real pig's ear of something think quietly about whether there is anything you can do to put it right. If you chewed someone off – particularly if they didn't really deserve it – ask yourself whether a quick 'sorry' will help. There's nothing like being seen as big enough to apologise for pushing up your stock in other people's estimation. But beyond that just let it go. Today will be better and in a week's time hardly anyone will remember what it was all about anyway.

## Z – ZOOS

AVOID THEM UNLESS, of course, you have young children and they are desperate to go. Indeed, unless you are in Defra and have to know about them, avoid all animals. Try not to be photographed with them – it's a gift for the *Private Eye* cover. And remember they'll only ever lose you votes, never gain you any. Stick to people. It's safer in the long run.

CHAPTER 6

# THE PERMANENT SECRETARY

*Precision, speed, unambiguity, knowledge of the files, continuity, discretion, unity, strict subordination, reduction of friction and of material and personal costs – these are raised to the optimum point in the strictly bureaucratic administration.*

MAX WEBER (1864–1920)

NOW THAT YOU'RE A SECRETARY of State, you can if you choose roam wide and deep in your department. You can get involved with any decision, however small. No one here can countermand you. You're in charge of developing the strategy. Communicating the strategy. Devising policy. Liaising with stakeholders. Getting on with colleagues. Accounting to Parliament. What could be better?

There's just one snag. Being a Secretary of State is just like being a chief executive, except with one rather important difference – it's not actually your job to run the organisation. Secretaries of State fail in many ways, but one of the most common is to think they're managers. You don't have the time (how many chief executives need to appear on the media at least once a day, make a speech most days, and spend two days a week working away from headquarters doing a completely different job as a constituency MP?). And even if you could find a way of working thirty hours a day, you almost certainly haven't got the necessary management skills.

Moreover, the machine won't cope with another quasi-Permanent Secretary, except one who can't be contradicted, and tends not to turn up to half of the necessary meetings. It would be like pouring diesel into a petrol engine.

Though, actually, that's not the biggest problem. The biggest problem is that even if you tried to be in charge, you would still be second in command on bureaucratic matters. The Permanent Secretary is ... well ... permanent. He or she is the one who decides who gets promoted. The one who has the time and (you hope) the skills to run the place. And the one who'll probably be here long after you leave (if you doubt that look at that other row of photographs – the one outside the Permanent Secretary's office of all their predecessors. What you realise instantly is there are far fewer of them than there are photos of your predecessors as Secretary of State).

Realise all this, and you may even feel a great weight lifted off your shoulders. Because another way of looking at this job split is that you make all the decisions and they do all the heavy lifting.

Also, you need them on your side. One Cabinet member known to us both objected to the Permanent Secretary they were being offered. They rang a Cabinet colleague – not a politician known for being in the pocket of the mandarins. His reaction was a surprise – 'You've got to swallow it. If you block a Perm Sec, you'll never get anything done in Whitehall again.'

As it happens we don't entirely share that view, as you will see at the end of this chapter. But there is no doubt that you don't want to fall out with the Wednesday Morning Meeting – the real shadow Cabinet, where Permanent Secretaries meet every week. They won't be out to get you – but if you lose credibility and goodwill, then it's diesel in the engine time again. They can raise their eyebrows all over Whitehall. They'll read your spending submissions critically. They'll assume that someone else will be in charge pretty soon.

And if that's not depressing, here's maybe a worse thought – your Permanent Secretary is the executor of your legacy. At some point, a few months or years away, a new minister will be sitting in your old office. If you convinced the department to like your policies, or even developed them together, they're much more likely to continue after you've gone. The first submission to your successor may defend your pet project rather than just automatically putting it in the savings column ('an innovative idea ... but early evidence disappointing').

So, while you're rushing from the TV studio to the Chamber, stopping off to show the leader of your council round Westminster Hall, the Permanent Secretary will be back in the department, running it. How should you both work together?

Like Siamese twins, if you can. You can disagree in private. But show a united front to the world. Division at the top is manna to a recalcitrant civil servant. If they've been over-ruled by the Permanent Secretary, they can try their luck with the minister. If they can't be bothered, they can let a disagreement fester. If they want to take a risk, they'll be worried that neither will stand up for them if things go wrong. The civil service is a machine that runs on process and decisions. Simply put, if you and the Permanent Secretary disagree, then no one is deciding.

Some tips. Meet every week as we have already said. Just you, your Principal Private Secretary and the Permanent Secretary. Not a long meeting, but the most important one of the week. You get to tell the Permanent Secretary what matters. You get to raise problems. They get to raise problems. You get to look them in the eye and ask for their support. They get to look you in the eye and ask for yours. The meeting symbolises and realises your joint leadership of the department. The Principal Private Secretary will also get to understand the dynamics at the top of the department – what it is you want to do and how you feel things are going.

And don't be afraid to enlist the help of your Principal Private Secretary. Most think they're primarily policy advisers. They're wrong – they're mostly marriage counsellors. It will feel like they live with you twenty-four hours a day. As far as your Permanent Secretary and you go, their job is to anticipate disagreements, defuse rows, calm feelings, raise flags, and remind you both of what you've promised to do. If you've got different views, they try to find a compromise. And if there's no compromise, they try to make sure that whoever wins, the other one isn't undermined or humiliated. Not many people can manage all of that – but if you find such a Private Secretary, don't let them go. (More of this later in our chapter on private office.)

Next, we need to deal with Sir Humphrey. Sad though it is to puncture one of the world's most enduring caricatures, in our experience Permanent Secretaries, whatever may have been the case a few years ago, just aren't like that. True, they come in different shapes and sizes. Some are – dare it be said – better than others but very few of them are ironic grandees looking with disdain at the amateurish efforts of their Secretaries of State. They also come now from a wider range of backgrounds. Plenty of policy specialists make it to the top – though in theory they should now also have some management on their CV. Some make their way up that way – people who started in a labour exchange and climbed all the way up the department. A few outsiders have even got in – mostly ex-local authority chief executives. Some spooks, some Treasury high-flyers.

If they're wise, they realise that Permanent doesn't mean Omnipotent. Business people are constantly getting to the top of organisations with gaps in their skills – the sales genius who is embarrassed to admit they can't read a balance sheet, the specialist in one industry who suddenly gets headhunted for another one. If they are wise, they use any time they have before their first day in charge to plug any gaps – either through coaching or team-building. So too in Whitehall – the best Permanent Secretaries are often at the centre of a small eco-system – they have their trusted sources of advice on key policy areas, their go-to fixer, the finance person they trust to understand the numbers and squirrel away pots of money for rainy days.

So, how do you split up the job?

We've already agreed that it's their job to run the department. But there's a snag – the doctrine of ministerial responsibility. In theory, if someone loses a tax disc in Dunfermline, it's your fault. But the practice has overtaken the theory. When tax discs disappear these days, it's Permanent Secretaries that resign, not ministers. That fact has electrified the Permanent Secretary network – the moment when the Chief Executive of HMRC resigned over the loss of the Child Benefit database was perhaps the most important since Michael Howard's dismissal of the then head of the Prison Service. Every Permanent Secretary across Whitehall turned away from the 24-hour news and vowed they wouldn't be next.

Apart from the second-order consequence that not much data was shared for a few months, that moment kicked off a transformation in accountability that is still underway today – namely that management accountability is emerging out from under the protective petticoats of ministerial responsibility. The signs of this change are proliferating – Permanent Secretaries are held accountable by Select Committees. The head of the civil service gives interviews. Crises like the border fiasco claim the head of the Border Agency, not of the Home Secretary. The Public Accounts Committee strikes terror in official minds, to the glee of political ones.

Some still contest this new settlement, and argue that the whole system is built on the fulcrum of ministerial responsibility. However, we believe that it is possible to keep ministerial accountability to Parliament while creating stronger management accountability for results. If you're still reading we set out our thoughts more fully in Part II on lessons learned.

But back to your weekly meeting. You and your Permanent Secretary will spend much of the agenda discussing problems at the interface between you. Benefit processing times are up? Is money or management the cause? Your meeting with the Chancellor? What's the absolute minimum outcome you and the department need? If you use these meetings well, the Permanent Secretary can take your shared agenda to the departmental management board that is likely to be their next meeting of the day.

Some Secretaries of State may not see their Permanent Secretary much more than that. Others will wonder why they keep on appearing in every meeting. For our money, the former is too hands-off, the latter a sign of insecurity. A confident Permanent Secretary knows that they don't have to be in every meeting – and indeed knows that they will devalue the currency if they are.

Instead, you'll want them to come to the main meetings on your key priorities (which now are also theirs). Again, don't contradict each other in public, but let the discussion flow and encourage dissent, before you sum up clearly.

The Permanent Secretary is also the go-to person about people. That might well be a wise piece of advice on what to do about an unruly junior minister, but it could also be about a recalcitrant official. Of course, politicians don't hire and fire civil servants, but any Permanent Secretary worth their salt is going to want their stars on the politicians' main policies, and will want to resolve any breakdown in relations. Make sure, though, that you let your Permanent Secretary do the moving – and be seen to.

But what if, despite all your best efforts, you just can't make it work? If mutual trust breaks down? If the truth is that you would prefer to see almost anyone in your office rather than the Permanent Secretary?

The first rule is not to rush at it. The risks for you of being seen to fall out with your Permanent Secretary are substantial.

So if you've fallen out big time over a particular issue, if you've had a real row, let the dust settle. Think whether a 'clear the air' meeting a few days later might help. Talk to your Principal Private Secretary. Talk to your lead non-executive director. But almost certainly to no one else. If an olive branch is offered think hard about taking it. Without compromising your authority think whether you can extend one also. In the meantime resist the very real temptation to let your dissatisfaction become more widely known; it will be the talk of the department before you've even put the receiver down. And if, by whatever means, you sense that there is a way forward, don't be afraid to grasp it. It is sometimes only after a real breakdown that real trust can be created.

If, however, in the very final analysis, you are utterly clear in your own mind that there has to be a change, then be prepared to bite the bullet. Talk to the head of the civil service and Cabinet Secretary, and as soon as you can, talk to the Permanent Secretary. They deserve to hear it from you, not from others. Next do all in your power to help a change to take place with civility and dignity. The Permanent Secretary's colleagues may well forgive you for wanting to make a change – indeed privately some may share some of your frustrations – but they won't forgive you, whatever they may think privately, if they think that the Permanent Secretary is being humiliated by you or your advisers.

But let's not end this chapter on such a gloomy note. Most Secretaries of State and most Permanent Secretaries manage to work together really well and, when they do, their departments can really motor. And you never know; one day you might find yourselves writing a book together.

## CHAPTER 7

# THE MEDIA

*Burke said there were Three Estates in Parliament; but, in the Reporters' Gallery yonder, there sat a Fourth Estate more important far than they all.*

THOMAS CARLYLE (1795–1881)

MOST MINISTERS, IF THEY ARE being frank, would probably concede that trying to manage the media is one of their biggest challenges and one that takes up a huge amount of time and effort. Sometimes, of course, it works. You will die for those memorable days when you are able to get across to the public precisely the message you want to communicate and the responses on the day – from the traditional media as well as the new forms of instant social media – are all positive, with the highly supportive editorial in *The Times* the icing on the cake. You can bask in the praise of your colleagues in Parliament and in government for the excellent job you are doing. If things have gone particularly well, you can even consider accepting the invitation to go on *Newsnight* – a task usually delegated to one of your junior ministers. But enjoy such days for their rarity value alone. Most of the time it will feel much more like a hard slog and on the really bad days it will be wholly down to you (or just occasionally your colleagues in government) to defend the badly formulated or poorly executed policy which cannot be brushed aside by you or your media advisers. There is nothing as lonely as the Secretary of State's office on the morning you wake up to the headlines from hell.

Moreover, the job of media management has just got a whole lot more complicated with the dramatic spread of social media. When the politician amongst the two of us first entered government in 1998 there was no Twitter. There wasn't much blogging. True, ministers then had to try and come to terms with the rise of the 24-hour news culture and the almost endless appetite for stories – whereas now this looks like the least of a minister's worries. One of the consequences of this rapid development in media technology has been to make the traditional ways of managing the media look less and less effective. In those happy days of the late 1990s ministerial spin-doctors would 'explain' the minister's thinking to an audience of journalists eager to understand what the minister really meant to say and why he was saying it. Now, whatever you say is instantly the subject of tweets and blogs providing a virtually uncontrollable source of views and commentary which the spin-doctor is powerless to influence. Many politicians – to say nothing of their civil servants – are only beginning to understand the significance of these new outlets for the spread of messages and stories. But this is what the future looks like. The traditional media – newspapers, TV and radio – are still hugely important forms of communication but the social media are without doubt the new kids on the block. When it comes to political messaging using social media, we are only beginning to understand its full implications and the best way to harness its considerable power. Caution is not a bad watchword and this applies particularly to outlets like Twitter. It can be an amazingly effective medium which can itself influence how the mainstream media report a story or development, but it can also frequently be the source of toe-curling embarrassment unless someone you trust is exercising effective editorial control of your tweets. And of course the real value of twittering is lost if it becomes obvious that your tweets have no personal authenticity.

So you would be right to assume from the outset that perhaps your most important job as a minister is to be absolutely on top of your personal and departmental communications. You are, after all, there to tell the public what you are trying to achieve and why you want to change things for the better. And when you become a Secretary of State that is a job you cannot delegate to anyone else. Your job is not only to accept the laurels but to take the punishment too. And there is going to be plenty of the latter to go around. So here are some thoughts on how to minimise the bad days and, hopefully, enjoy more of the good ones.

First, a healthy dose of humility will help. By the time you become a minister you probably think you know all there is to know about handling the media. After all, you have been dealing with them from the very first moment you became a parliamentary candidate and for all of the time you have been in the House. What can be different now that you're a minister? The simple answer is everything. You are now the person under the spotlight and every aspect of your personal as well as political life will be under scrutiny. Nothing you do – from the most important to the most utterly trivial – will be off limits as far as the media are concerned.

To start at the traditional end, the Lobby correspondents – the political journalists whose job it is to record the ups, the downs, the intrigues and the contortions of the Westminster village – continue to be extremely important relationships to manage and nurture in no small part because your departmental media team are likely to think, rightly, that most of this falls under the 'political' label. So it has to be down to you to work at these relationships, not least because they impact so directly on your political reputation. Pending the result of the next general election it is these journalists who will form both judge and jury on your performance and therefore on your career as a Cabinet minister. At the same time how much time and effort you want to spend on these relationships has to be down to you. We have seen ministers spend almost their entire life courting the Lobby to the detriment of their departments – often with almost nothing to show for it. At the other extreme, some outstanding ministers, like Ken Clarke, seemed to be able to spend almost no time at all on this endeavour and instead got on with the job of running their departments very effectively without apparently losing anything in the process. That may, of course, be because they were the rare example of those very few ministers who, without undermining collective responsibility, manage, like Ken Clarke, to speak in sentences which ordinary people can understand, devoid of double negatives and circumlocutions. If only most ministers had that ability.

Of course now that you are responsible for a department, your media remit will run very much further than the interests of the Lobby. At the other end of the spectrum, the trade or specialist press that covers your ministerial portfolio will now be following your every move with rapt attention. They are all too easy to belittle but you should never underestimate their importance. *Sewage and Waste Management World* may not be a household name publication but if they decide that you're either wilfully ignoring them or, worse, positively slighting them, they may have more influence than you might think. Conversely, if they decide that you're that rare beast – a competent minister in their field of interest – what they write and tweet can find its way into the mainstream media and the wider body politic much more often than you might imagine. Moreover, failure to manage this avenue of communications can turn something which appears at first sight to be utterly trivial into a front-page story very quickly. So take advice from your professional media team on how to manage these journalists who they almost certainly know much better than you do. Accept their advice to do an interview from time to time. And accept that you might not know the answer to everything. Your department's network of contacts in this respect is much more powerful than you think.

More generally, it's fundamentally important for you to decide how you want your media relations to be managed within the department. As Secretary of State your political co-author preferred to work with a dedicated and trusted press officer who managed all of his media relations (apart from those which were strictly political) rather than work with several different people handling separate areas of policy. In this way the Press Secretary could speak with absolute authority and a clear understanding of what the Secretary of State wanted to do and why. Of course, if you have that modern-day phenomenon of a 'media Spad' (for the uninitiated reader, a special adviser who concentrates wholly or mainly on your media coverage), you need to try hard to ensure that they have a good working relationship with the head of your civil service press office. Where the two work well together – and there are without doubt two different jobs to be done – your media handling will seriously benefit. But where there is squabbling and infighting it can be hugely damaging.

Be prepared too to put in the work before a big announcement. The first golden rule is not to try and make it up as you go along. Left to their own devices, your officials will miraculously provide you with dozens of pages of 'Q&As' which will seek to provide answers to every conceivable question anyone might possibly ask you about your new policy and to explain why any conceivable criticism is misguided ('Q. Doesn't the fact that you said only last year that you would introduce this policy only over your dead body and yet you are now doing so indicate that this is the biggest U-turn of this Parliament? A. This is, of course, a wholly different policy responding to wholly different circumstances.') It is very easy to ignore these documents and to regard them simply as annoying bundles of paper. Needless to say, very few of these questions ever actually get asked but it is nonetheless important that you go through the detail of all this material to try to spot the real nasties that could find their way into the media. Your policy officials have the prime responsibility for preparing all of this but your private office can help provide further reassurance as to its quality and relevance. Having gone through it you can more confidently concentrate on the big picture and the broad messages – but beware still; every big picture is made up of tiny brush strokes and if even one of these is not right then the overall effect you want to create can be compromised.

Second, recognise that effective communication around a big announcement doesn't happen by chance. It happens because it has been properly planned and executed. It is fundamental to good communications to ensure that every new policy announcement also comes with a sensible communications plan which covers all the main verbal and visual messages you want to convey on the day. And don't think you can happily leave this to others while you take a well-earned night off, having finally worked your way through the actual policy. You need to take personal responsibility for agreeing these arrangements and you will almost certainly want to involve your special advisers in this process as well. They are, after all, your extra pairs of eyes and ears and their own political antennae should be a trusted source of advice. But in the end no one but you can ensure that you end up with a plan that you are comfortable with. There is nothing worse than that sinking feeling of finding yourself being transported on the day of your big announcement to some distant and unattractive location, wondering who on earth agreed to such a ridiculous place for the launch. Or finding that the organisation hosting your visit doesn't actually agree with the policy you're announcing and have put out a press notice to that effect. No amount of shouting at your press officer – or alternatively sitting in sullen silence – on the car journey back to your office can disguise the fact that you will know that you should have gone through all this much more thoroughly in advance. You must take responsibility.

Third, remember that, while you may think that your announcement is the only worthwhile show in town, you will not be the only person in government trying to manage the media that day or that week. In government there is always a plethora of news stories emerging every day. No. 10 will want to be informed of, and have the final say over, what media messages it wants to highlight and for your part you have to decide whether you want to be a team player or not. Our own view is very clear; government is a team sport, not a festival of prima donnas. Someone has to hold the ring and No. 10 is the obvious repository for this responsibility. And if that sometimes works against you, get over it. Remember, you are part of a wider project. Your horizons need to go much further than your own immediate departmental interests. What you can, and must do, however, is ensure that No. 10 know what you are planning and when. Just as they can be incredibly irritating if they ask you to play second fiddle to another colleague, or even to the PM, they can be incredibly helpful if they understand your objectives and row in behind them. They can provide vital turbo power to your announcement.

Fourth, remember that yours will not be the only voice which is going to be heard when you launch your new policy. Others are going to get the chance to comment as well and not all of these comments are going to be well informed or helpful. Preparing the ground beforehand for any important announcement with key organisations or commentators is a pre-requisite. If at all possible share your thinking and the rationale that underpins your new strategy with the key external opinion formers and make sure you take the time to do it properly. Your junior ministers can help but in the end there is no substitute for much of this coming from you. At the same time it is always a good idea to make clear to these contacts what it is that you are not proposing to do as well as what you are. Dealing with confusion on the day as to what it is that you have or haven't announced will not just be the source of much wasted energy but will seriously blunt the impact of your announcement. And if all of this really can't be done in advance, for reasons of confidentiality or security, then at least make the calls as soon as you possibly can after the event.

Finally, think through what those who are likely to come out against your new policy are likely to say. You will need to be able to respond to the stories they are generating. With sufficient thought and planning you may be able to pre-empt at least some of their main lines of attack, or appropriate a few of their best lines for yourself. This is something your press team and Spads should be on top of but again they will need your time and input if they are to plan your department's communications in an effective way.

In the end, of course, in this, as in every area of managing the media, there is no magic formula for success. Successful communication is a combination of your own personal style and authority mixed with careful preparation. And even where you follow all these rules and tips you are still, over your time as Secretary of State, going to experience some truly awful days. Some of these will be down to you – you will have done or said something that has horribly backfired. Others will be the result of some hideous cock-up in your department. The rest will simply be down to events and fate: the bomb attack, the leak, the train crash. On days like these there are, however, still some basic rules to try and follow.

If you are dealing with a bad news story emanating from your own department, or a breaking news story affecting it, it is usually a good idea to say nothing until you have established all of the facts. Resist the temptation to get in front of the cameras until you are sure of your ground. Responding too quickly without all of the necessary information at your fingertips will only make matters much worse. Establishing the true facts will be the job of your senior officials and of the Permanent Secretary in particular. Get these officials involved right at the beginning of the exercise and be clear about what you want. Once the facts have been established, and when it is clear that your department is at the centre of the storm or the allegation, you need to make one fundamental decision – whether you can go on the offensive or whether you need to say sorry. If the facts are as bad as they appear then you will need to decide how to apologise and to make sure your apology is believed and accepted. Do this with as much grace as you can muster. Never create the impression that although you are saying sorry you don't really mean it or you don't think it is fair that you are being asked to eat humble pie. This will only defeat the whole purpose of the exercise and you will be back in the midst of the storm you are trying to escape from. The purpose of any apology is to try and draw a line under a bad news story – not to give it fresh legs. It is possible that your apology might have serious personal consequences for you or some of your officials – that is a different matter which we explore later on. Our own very strong view is that the Secretary of State should accept responsibility for the failures of his or her department and not seek to blame individuals within it.

If you are able to get on the front foot – and the facts support a different version of events than the one presented in the media – then your essential task is to let the facts speak for themselves. You may feel indignant, even traduced, by the media coverage and may want to convey a sense of anger at the outrageous distortions of the press. It is generally a good idea, however, to keep these sorts of emotions under wraps. The public are generally not interested in how you feel, will probably have little sympathy for you in any case, but do want to know what has actually happened (or not as the case may be). They will form their own view, so make sure they have the real picture, undistorted by any emotions you might feel tempted to transmit. Going on to the offensive on a bad news story can be a brilliant tactic – on the basis that the facts support such a move – and you may want to involve No. 10 and others in mounting your counter-attack. A strong kinetic response is always a good option when you are fighting a rearguard action.

If the bad day has been caused not simply by events, or by a departmental failure, but by your own behaviour, then only you can resolve the problem through an effective apology, and your department will probably not be able to provide much by way of help. In these cases genuine contrition will be necessary. Speed will be of the essence and may be the only way for you to escape further punishment. In the extreme case there may be no escape, in which case you need to plan your exit with as much dignity as time allows. More on this later.

Above all, when these bad days happen (and they will) avoid displays of temper and bad grace at all costs. Take the blows as graciously as you can, however painful they might be. It is not the criticism of others you should fear, it is your own decisions that matter the most and by which you will ultimately be judged. Get these right and, by and large, the rest will follow. Above all, try and keep a sense of proportion. Some interviews will bomb. Some photographs will make you look like a cross between a gibbering wreck and a Martian zombie so that even your adoring partner will hide the paper under the coffee table. None of this stuff, at the end of the day, really counts for very much and it is far more ephemeral than you might think when you are caught in the cross-wires. What will prove much more damaging to your prospects as a Cabinet minister is the perception that you are simply not on top of your job, because at that point you cease to be of any value to the government. Bad days will test your judgement to the limit. No amount of good communication will ever disguise this bald reality.

CHAPTER 8

# SPECIAL ADVISERS

*The adjective 'special' in front of the word 'advisers' performs the same role as when the same adjective is displayed in front of 'education'.*

DANIEL FINKELSTEIN, *THE TIMES*, 2009

## LEIGH LEWIS

SLIGHTLY TRICKY ONE this, given that there are rather a lot of present and past special advisers out there, all of whom we would love to buy this book. Let's be clear, therefore, that without special advisers the entire system of government in the UK would undoubtedly fracture, thus without doubt putting at risk the future of the Western world if not the future of all life as we know it on this planet.

The strange thing is that, while the planet and the Western

world might somehow get over the shock, it is quite hard now to conceive of government in this country without the presence of special advisers. And you – Secretary of State – are undoubtedly going to want some in any event, so here goes with a few thoughts on the subject from the perspective of a former mandarin. If you desperately want an alternative perspective from a former Secretary of State then you will find John's later in this chapter.

The first questions are how many and who they should be. The answer to the first question should be simple: two. That has been laid down by successive Prime Ministers and there are no exceptions; or none officially anyway; or not that many. The truth, however, is that if you desperately want to get in a third (a fourth starts looking very greedy and five or more will get you into serious trouble) there are probably ways and means, such as appointing one of the three as an 'expert' adviser. But you need to proceed with some care and you will have to agree that only the two full-blown special advisers (or 'Spads' as they are now universally known inside Whitehall) can do the really political stuff like attending party conferences and writing your speeches for party events. You might well want in any event to stick to the regulation two and enjoy the luxury of a totally clear conscience.

The question of who may not be quite so easy. You may well be absolutely certain of the answer in which case this is a non-issue but, even then, it is probably worth spending just a moment or two asking yourself if you really are sure that the people you have in mind, however long they have worked with you and however close to them you are, will really be the people best able to help you succeed in the strange world of Whitehall. That may be a question about their policy range and breadth – the world's greatest expert on a single issue may struggle when confronted with the bewildering range and complexity of subjects with which any Whitehall department has to deal – or it may be one about their style – the classic *The Thick of It* gorilla may have been useful to you in the past but is likely at some stage to come to grief, and possibly bring you down with them, in a world where such behaviours are widely regarded as simply unacceptable.

If, by contrast, you have not got the answer to 'who' already sorted, then it is worth thinking through what it is you want from your Spads before you go any further. Is your key consideration to have someone who can watch your political back, and make sure you don't alienate the party, while you get on with the job of running your bit of the government? Is it someone who can help you deal with the mass of issues and papers your department will load upon you and help you spot the political hot potato your civil servants are ignoring? Or is it someone who is genuinely expert on the two or three really big issues that matter the most to you and who can help you drive them through? And do you want one of your Spads to handle the political side of your contacts with the media that your departmental press team can't (the 'Media Spad' role described in our chapter on the media) – something which has become increasingly de rigueur in recent years? Depending on the answers to these questions you will probably be looking for rather different people.

Let's also go back for a moment in this context to the issue of behaviours. The great majority of Spads make it their business to get on good terms not just with your ministerial team and your key political and other contacts, but also with your civil servants. They don't set themselves up to be your shock troops; they don't spend their entire lives telling you how stupid some of your civil servants are – though even the very best can't resist doing so occasionally – and they don't spend their time telling your senior civil servants in words of one syllable where they can put themselves and their submissions. But some do and you don't need me to remind you of some of the more recent celebrated cases. You may be tempted to think, of course, that this last may not be such a bad approach and that someone needs to put a bit of welly about, but you would almost certainly be wrong. It is generally not a question of whether it will end in tears but when – and you will probably have no control over the latter. So while you do not have to hire genuine five-star angels as your special advisers you would be well advised to avoid the real five-star thugs.

Alright; one way or another you've appointed your Spads and No. 10 has blessed their appointment (don't forget, by the way, that you do need the Prime Minister's formal approval before you can go ahead). What next? How do you want them to operate? And should you be laying down any ground rules as to how they should do so?

The first thing to say is that, used well, your Spads can be a real asset to you. The enduring *Yes Minister* image of your Spad being despatched to the basement of a social security office in Clapham is genuinely in the past. You may be surprised to find that your department is not institutionally resistant to your Spads or to everything that they propose. On the contrary, most of your civil servants – and certainly the best of them – will have long ago worked out that there is real advantage in working as closely with them as possible.

They use them to try to find out what is likely to be politically acceptable to you and what will not; they float the options that they want to put to you to see if there are aspects of them that they have not taken into account; they will often talk to them about whether they can get political agreement from other departments on the political adviser net that they can't get from their official opposite numbers in the departments concerned. In short, they want them inside the tent if at all possible.

That is, almost certainly, something you should encourage. Of course, there will be times when you will want to look to your Spads for a different perspective – a second opinion if you will. And you do need them to tell you when, in their view, the official advice coming up to you is simply wrong. But, in general, you will be better served by their working with your civil servants than working against them. There is nothing quite as powerful, or actually enjoyable, as your ministerial team, your Spads and your civil servants pulling together to help drive through something of real importance to you and the department. You need to make clear to your Spads that that is how, overwhelmingly, you want them to work.

Of course, it takes two to tango. You are entitled to expect in return that the department will not freeze out your Spads; that they will give them the information they need; that they will, as a matter of course, copy all important submissions and papers to them; and that they will treat them as trusted insiders not suspicious outsiders. If you suspect that this isn't happening you need one of 'those' conversations with your Permanent Secretary, probably with no one else in the room.

You also need to think about how you want your Spads to operate in relation to their counterparts in other departments. In that context not everyone realises just how strong the Whitehall special adviser net is. Inevitably special advisers spend a lot of time talking to each other. Many of them have bonds of friendship and shared experience which date back over many years. Numerically they are a very small group in a huge government and, consciously or unconsciously, they look to each other for a good deal of mutual support. They talk about all of you just as you talk about each other.

Now that can have its drawbacks. If you want to operate Fortress DfT, DWP or FCO in which no paper, idea or proposal ever leaves the ramparts other than with your express permission then your Spads are either going to be seriously emasculated, if they follow your orders, or facing charges of treachery if they don't. And even if you operate in a much more relaxed way than that there can still be times when you find that your Spads are having conversations or floating ideas that you might prefer they didn't. But, overwhelmingly, you have much more to gain than to lose from letting your Spads make full use of the special adviser network. Particularly if they are good they can sometimes do the deals you can't and find the compromises you couldn't or didn't want to contemplate openly. And they have the great advantage that the fellow Spads they are talking to will have the trust of their ministerial bosses and immediate access to them. So if the Chancellor is declining to take your phone calls and your private office is getting the cold shoulder ('of course the Chancellor would be more than happy to talk to your Secretary of State; it's just that he's taken up completely today with the President of the World Bank's visit') then your Spads may be your best route in.

One area, though, where you may decide you will in general be safer not having your Spads giving you advice is where you have to exercise quasi-judicial functions, such as whether to call in a planning application or intervene in a deportation decision. Those are the decisions – particularly susceptible to being judicially reviewed – where you do not want to, or to be seen to, allow party political considerations to influence the outcome. It may be deeply frustrating to your Spads, and inconvenient to you, not to have them in the room or reading the papers in such instances, but on the day when your every action is being reviewed in painstaking detail by the Court of Appeal you are likely to be profoundly grateful for their not having been involved. This really is one area where you need the advice, and agreement, of your Permanent Secretary, if you want your special advisers involved at all.

One final thought of a rather different kind in this handy advice column is this; talk to your Spads all you like and make clear that they have a standing invitation to all your key meetings. The more they know what's really motivating and worrying you the better. But don't let them become the guardians of your door deciding who you should and shouldn't see, and what you should and shouldn't read. Not only will that hack off your senior officials big time – to say nothing of your own private office – but it can leave you increasingly isolated from the range of views and opinions you need to hear in coming to decisions. The best ministers are almost always the ones who want to hear the debate and, within reason, give everyone their say before making up their own mind.

So there you go; all you need to know about special advisers in one easy to read summary. But if, strangely, you do still feel the need for another perspective, here it is...

## JOHN HUTTON

WELL, CLASSIC MANDARIN stuff if I may say so, even if – as it happens – I agree with a good deal of it. But let me give you my own perspective untouched by Sir Humphrey.

Appointing your special advisers will be one of the most important decisions you ever make as a Secretary of State. If you get it right, you will be a more effective minister and better able to bring about the changes you want to make. A good Spad can help you come to the right decisions – ones that work both politically as well as from a policy perspective, which is the ministerial sweet spot you will always be looking to hit. The importance of your Spads is confirmed by one simple fact – the only people in your department that you are allowed to appoint yourself are your Spads. That should tell you all you need to know.

So choosing the right people to act for you in this role is absolutely critical. Many Secretaries of State will already have worked closely with party officials or with policy experts in their shadow teams. They can make excellent Spads, and this is particularly true if the all-important relationship of trust and confidence has already been established because it is central to the very nature of the role. But there can also be considerable merit in going outside the narrow confines of party politics, in the search for either policy expertise or for a wider skill set altogether. Simon Stevens was an outstanding Spad for Frank Dobson, Alan Milburn and Tony Blair and came into government directly from the NHS. John Williams, who worked for me in DWP, Business and Defence, was recruited from the CBI after a successful career in the private sector. Without John's support I doubt whether I could have done half the things we managed to achieve in government. Paul Corrigan, an academic by background, worked really well with John Reid at Health. All these people brought maturity and judgement into their role as Spads – qualities that are just as important in my view as in-depth policy experience.

So herein lies the rub. What we are really talking about in this context is the sharing of executive power. There should never be any doubt about who gets to make decisions in government. It is the exclusive job of ministers. When it comes to exercising executive power, civil servants clearly occupy a central function in providing advice and support. But in our system of government, so do Spads. They occupy a perfectly legitimate and proper role and must be given the space and the opportunity to contribute to the advice ministers receive. The department must ensure that this happens. If it is not happening then you need to make sure that that changes.

In an ideal world, a Spad should work as a fully integrated part of the team advising ministers. Hopefully a consensus can be reached. But life isn't always like that – and neither is politics. Sometimes there will be disagreements, but that does not spell the end of the world as we know it. Disagreements will not always be a bad thing. They can equally be a sign that your Spad is doing what he or she is paid to do – providing an independent source of advice to you about the policy you should be following. That can be hugely important, especially if you are not happy with the status quo and want to get things moving more quickly or in a different direction.

Constant disagreements may of course spell something different – namely that relationships between your officials and your Spads have become fractured. In that case you and your Permanent Secretary need to try to resolve the underlying issues. Where these sorts of problems do exist they cannot be ignored or shuffled under the carpet.

Media Spads present a different set of challenges and it is here that most of the real problems have tended to arise. It is entirely proper for a Secretary of State to have the support of a full-time media Spad given the fact that the department's own press team cannot help you manage party political issues. But how many times have we seen the role of the media Spad create real problems for ministers, and indeed for governments? Your media Spad owes their loyalty to you as their Secretary of State but that must never be allowed to turn into a free for all where the needs of the government play second fiddle to other agendas. And nor should you countenance some of the behaviours that a few media Spads have adopted in the past. You have to set the tone and style of your relationships with the media and your Spad must work within the guidelines you establish as well as within the clear rules that now exist in the code of conduct. My own media Spad, John Woodcock, followed an exemplary ethical code when he worked for me. Far from being a hindrance to him in his work on my behalf, it helped him do his job even more effectively in my eyes. And there are many other similar examples.

But be careful – there is no Secretary of State more important than the government itself. Your media Spad needs to understand this simple rule of politics or you will have to deal with the consequences.

So there you have it; you can re-read the 'Sir Humphrey' version if you want. But never forget that this is one area where what really matters is what you want.

## CHAPTER 9

# MINISTERS

*Politics is perhaps the only profession for which no preparation is thought necessary.*

ROBERT LOUIS STEVENSON (1850–1894)

IN GENERAL THE ADVICE IN our book is intended, rather presumptuously, for a newly appointed Secretary of State. But we thought that we might, at least in this chapter, say something aimed at ministers more generally. If nothing else it may help the sales figures.

'Minister'; the very word is intoxicating. And so is all the paraphernalia: ministerial cars, ministerial boxes (they really are red, by the way, but a real pain if you lose the key), ministerial private offices, ministerial Parliamentary Private Secretaries, ministerial drivers (though going out of fashion a bit as their costs get revealed in response to Freedom of Information requests), and the ministerial code (we'll come back to this later; not good if you're found in breach of it).

And now you are one. Or an even more senior one. Or, finally, the Secretary of State. And don't give us all that guff about the only thing that matters being the interests of the country and that you've got no interest in power for its own sake. Ever since you first thought about politics as a career you've dreamed about that day when the Prime Minister calls and offers you the post. And now it's happened. You were, of course, suitably modest in your conversation with the PM – 'if you believe I can serve, PM, then you will have my absolute support' – but inside you were shouting 'yippee; I've made it'. Or, at least, 'phew; I really thought I was for the boot after that less than inspired interview on *Newsnight* where even my friends avoided eye contact the next day'.

And make the most of the feeling. You've earned it. All those unbelievably dreary constituency events you've loyally attended; all those dinners (eating rubber chicken, as Michael Heseltine supposedly once described it) you've gone to on Friday nights when you'd have given anything just to curl up on the sofa with the children or watch the game on Sky; all those endless letters from obsessive constituents that you've responded to on Sunday evenings trying to find the fine line between telling them they're barking and losing their vote for ever, but not giving them any encouragement to keep writing. None of your civil servants have ever had to do any of that, and certainly not the Permanent Secretary who generally seems to regard anything to do with votes or voters as barely mentionable in polite society.

So you deserve the reward. It's what you've always wanted

and – let's put the cynics and the media back where they belong – you genuinely believe that you can make some things better and you're going to do your damnedest to do so.

Which means that, once the initial feeling of euphoria has worn off – and it won't take long – you need to think long and hard about what kind of minister you want to be and how you are going to try to end up succeeding rather than failing.

The first thing to say is that there is no magic formula for instant ministerial success. Some of the most unlikely candidates for high office have succeeded whereas some of those marked out by their own peers and the media as on their certain way to stardom have fallen by the wayside to such an extent that they have become virtual non-people within their own parties.

Some of this, of course, is down to pure luck. The best minister in the world is going to struggle if events simply conspire against them. If you're left holding the baby on the day your department loses the memory stick with half the country's tax records on it you're going to need to be a cross between Churchill and Einstein to turn that into a political success. And on the day when two inches of snow have turned the entire country into the world's largest car park the greatest Transport Minister in history is going to face calls for their resignation if they are not seen at the very least to be personally out with a shovel on the M25.

But there are some things that you can do which will increase the odds that you end up succeeding rather than failing. Apologies if what follows seems a bit Janet and John. But if you already know it all it will at least be welcome confirmation and, if you don't, well at least someone tried to give you some genuinely well-intentioned advice.

First, be prepared to work really hard. The media love the stereotype image of ministers living it up in the lap of luxury as they move from one starstruck restaurant to another leaving their constituents and the country to sink or swim. But the truth is that about 95 per cent of ministerial life is sheer slog and, if you want to succeed, you are going to have to work as hard probably as you've ever done in your life. We've stressed in an earlier chapter the importance of identifying, and then focusing relentlessly on, those very few things that you really want to make your top priorities. But that doesn't mean that you can simply ignore everything else. It may simply mean having to work even harder at times.

Different ministers have different working styles; some are simply quicker than others at absorbing issues and material. And, yes, you can tell your private office how you want notes and submissions to come to you and, if you still feel you're drowning under the weight, you can get them to put out pretty fearsome guidelines on how you are, and are not, prepared to work. And as we note elsewhere you can, and should, try and exercise some real control over your diary which, left to itself, your private office will fill up on a near 24/7 basis.

But even after doing all of this you can't avoid the work. Government departments are massive entities; they deal with everything from the most potentially far-reaching to the most unbelievably trivial. And words are their stock in trade. You can have them sent to you electronically rather than on paper; put on a maximum of two, three or four sides; specify the type size and have submissions go through your Spads before they reach you (though not, generally, a great idea) but in the end you are simply going to have to spend hours of every day reading lots of pretty dull and tedious stuff to the point where you understand it well enough to at least understand what it is you're being asked to decide. If you don't sooner or later you are going to get caught out and you're going to wish you had put in the time you needed. And you're going to have to do all this while simultaneously still dealing with all of your constituency obligations, to say nothing of the small matter of coping with the House and staying on top of your brief in that respect.

Second, managing your time. Now you're a minister, or an even more senior minister, kiss goodbye to any idea that you will have, or should somehow expect to have, large parts of the week which are simply for you. You can, of course, try to carve out some such periods – even your own private office, which has an uncanny knack of knowing where you are even when you have deliberately given them no clue whatsoever, will probably leave you alone between midnight and 6.00 a.m. – and there is nothing like cultivating a strong religious devotion – whether authentic or not – which allows you to bar all contact while you are supposedly paying allegiance to a higher authority. But for the most part simply accept that, for as long as you hold ministerial office, you have forfeited any real control over a great deal of your life outside.

And that will help. There will be any number of people, organisations, stakeholders (an interesting word on which views vary; it's a bit like Marmite – you either love it or hate it), constituents, lobbyists, pressure groups, journalists, to say nothing of fellow ministers and your own civil servants, who think they are absolutely entitled to your time. But that – more often than you might think – is all they want or expect. Yes, they will come through your door, or invite you through theirs, with an agenda, a wish list and a proposal for the next sixteen times they hope to see you. But many are, deep down, much more realistic than you might imagine; they know the constraints you are under; they know there's no money; they know that even if you say yes the Treasury or No. 10 may well say no. But what they really want is you; your time and your presence. They want to feel that they at least matter enough to see, and be seen by, a Minister of the Crown. If they can achieve that you may be pleasantly surprised at how well they speak of you to others and the media even if you haven't been able to do anything serious for them. Conversely, if they think that they're simply being given the cold shoulder their disdain, and even venom, for you will know no bounds.

As we note elsewhere when it comes to the Secretary of State it simply isn't survivable to meet with everyone who wants to see you unless you want to work 24/7 on a never-ending basis. But as a less senior minister the pressures are not quite as intense. So, however tedious it may seem, it may well be in your interests to agree to the meeting, or to take on the proposed speaking engagement, unless it is blatantly counter-productive to do so. And sometimes when you do, you can find that it's actually much more interesting, and occasionally even much more fun, to do so than you ever thought it would be.

Thirdly, in your quest for ministerial success, you need to think very carefully about the relationship you want to build with your civil servants, about which we have already said something in our earlier chapters and about whom we say more in the chapter that follows. Whether you like it or not they are going to dominate huge parts of your ministerial life. They are the people who operate the machine; they generally know a good deal more about each subject area for which you are responsible than you do; they are there to do your bidding and if they put their backs into it they can help you achieve remarkable things. But they can also be deeply frustrating, unimaginative and, sometimes, just not very good.

Or at least some can. The first thing to realise is that they span a huge range in terms of competence, experience and knowledge. The very best are quite simply outstanding. They are prepared to work every hour that God sends; are committed to delivering the very best product they can and have huge experience of how to make things happen. They can open doors in walls you didn't even think had doors in them. They can fashion the compromise between two seemingly irreconcilable positions. And they can be great fun to work with.

But they will also be wary. They've seen ministers come and go at a frequency which would have seemed laughable if it wasn't so serious. They've been chewed up and spat out by some of your predecessors who seemed to think it some kind of test of their machismo to humiliate them publicly. They've put their all into trying to deliver the ultimately undeliverable policy and then been publicly blamed when it ended in tears. And that's just the really good ones.

There is, of course, no one magic formula for dealing with your civil servants. But there are some pointers. The first is that the nicer you are to them, the more they will try to do for you. If you are as miserable as sin; if you constantly harangue and complain; if you look for the nearest person to blame at the first hint of trouble then don't be surprised if you get corresponding behaviours back. The second is that the safer you make it to tell you the truth, the more of the truth you will be told. It is sometimes only your civil servants who can see that you are driving the lorry over the cliff edge. But whether they will tell you that you are about to do so or not will depend in part on whether they think that they are going to be shot if they do. The third, pretty basic, pointer is simply to thank your civil servants when they do something well. Like most other human beings – and yes they are human beings – they react far better to praise than criticism.

Now you can probably see where this is going. There are two basic approaches: number one, the complete bastard; number two, the reasonable man or woman. Please take two minutes now to consider which you intend to be and then vote on your keypad.

Sorry, patronising and over-simplistic, of course. But nonetheless pretty fundamental. The best ministers recognise that their civil servants – or at least a good number of them – have genuinely valuable experience and insights. Treating that experience with respect doesn't have to slow things down and will generally lead to your decisions being thought through more thoroughly and your policies better designed. And your civil servants will respect a decision more if it has been made in the light of a serious discussion, even if you choose to discount some of what you've heard. In the end it is about mutual respect. Ministers will gain more respect if they themselves show respect for their civil servants.

Don't believe, by the way, that if you decide to head for the 'decent minister' corner it means that you have to put up with second rate in terms of quality, effort or commitment. You have an absolute right to expect the very best of which your civil servants are capable. But the irony is that when it is the decent minister who is the one saying that something simply isn't good enough it has a far more profound effect than when it can simply be dismissed as just the latest rant by someone who still wouldn't be satisfied if the Charge of the Light Brigade had been miraculously turned into the greatest military triumph since the Norman conquest.

Think too how you will behave on the bad days. It's easy to be utterly charming and gracious on the good days when everything's gone well, when even No. 10 are happy and when you've managed somehow to get some great coverage in the media. The real test is on the day when it's all gone pear-shaped, particularly when it's not remotely your fault but probably is the department's, and No. 10 are on the warpath for heads to roll.

If on those days you simply lash out in all directions while trying desperately to cover your own back, you will probably never regain any shred of trust from your civil servants. If it was indeed their fault they will know that they've screwed up and will generally be feeling utterly mortified as a result. They don't need you to tell them. What they will respect enormously, however, is if you make clear that you are going to take public responsibility for whatever has happened but you now need every ounce of support they can give you to try and remedy the situation. Nor does any of this mean that there is no need for an inquest into what happened and why; almost certainly there will need to be precisely that. But it does generally mean holding back on that until the immediate problem is resolved.

Fourth, and finally, it's worth saying a word on decisions. That is, ultimately, what ministers are there for: to take them. The trouble is that not all that many of them are self-evident and in all too many cases they involve deciding between the lesser of any number of evils. As you read through the classic ministerial submission – 'there are three options, minister (why always three?), one's mad, one's bad and the other is the only logical one to take despite all its self-evident disadvantages' – it is all too easy to lose the will to live.

There is always the option of taking no decisions. It's not completely mad either. From Elizabeth I onwards there have always been leaders whose fundamental approach has been to take no decision until the point when the decision effectively takes itself anyway. It was much easier to decide to resist if you'd just been invaded than to decide whether to launch the invasion yourself. And, as a tactic, it has something going for it. There are times when all of the available options are so fundamentally unattractive that not doing any of them can be the least worst option. And sometimes events do come to your rescue in ways that you couldn't have expected.

But Elizabeth I had the advantage of not living in an era of rolling 24/7 news coverage ('Breaking News: we're getting reports that Mary, Queen of Scots, has been seen being led to the scaffold at Fotheringay'); Freedom of Information requests ('it has been revealed today that the Queen has spent over 15,000 sovereigns on mascara over the last year in an apparently unsuccessful attempt to retain her youthful countenance'); and undercover exposés ('the News of the Court is alleging that Sir Francis Drake's recent decision to finish his game of bowls before tackling the Spanish Armada was taken as part of a betting scam involving a number of members of the English bowls team'). There are simply too many decisions that can't be put off to enable you to rest entirely on this tactic.

So how best to go about taking the decisions you clearly need or want to? Getting as many facts as you can is never a bad starting point and challenging any of them that seem flaky or counter-intuitive will give you a sense of how robust the arguments are. Having the arguments put to you face to face by your officials will often help you to clear your own mind. So too will asking your special advisers for their views, which can often be a healthy counterweight to the official machine. And talking to ministerial and other colleagues, both inside and outside the department, is very rarely wasted time if the issue warrants it.

But in the end simply doing what you think is right is generally a pretty good tactic. And recognising that, in the nature of politics, not every decision you take will turn out to have been the right one even if it seemed likely to be at the time. The only minister who never takes any bad decisions is the minister who never takes any decisions at all. And that is almost certainly far more fatal to a successful ministerial career than taking some decisions which turn out to be poor ones. So take the best decisions you can, think about them hard before you do so, take and listen to advice but, in the end, don't beat yourself up if you get some of them wrong.

Which leaves only the issue of the ministerial code, which we said at the outset we would say something more about. The code, which has actually been getting shorter rather than longer with successive redrafts over the years, sets out the ultimate list of 'dos' and 'don'ts' for ministers. It is a bit like the Ten Commandments though with a bit more room for judgement and some bits left out (it assumes, for example, that stealing is always wrong without making it explicit).

The very first thing to do is ask your private office to get you a copy and make sure it's the up-to-date one. The second is to read it. And the third – pretty important this one – is to abide by it – scrupulously. The problem, of course, is that it can still leave grey areas where the guidance is less than clear. In those cases it is almost always a very good idea to ask the Permanent Secretary's advice. Although the ultimate judgement has to be yours – and yours alone – the Permanent Secretary has generally seen it all before and will have an instinctive feel for what is right and wrong. And, in cases of real doubt, he or she can get advice from the expert team in the Cabinet Office who have seen all the cases over all the years when ministers ended up writing their resignation statements because they simply thought they could get away with it or, worse, didn't even realise there was a problem in the first place. And remember too that following the spirit of the code is every bit as important as following the letter. Remember some of those ministers in the past who had, on the advice of their accountants, stuck to the letter of the law in arranging their tax affairs but still found themselves damned for taking action which still looked to the average taxpayer like elaborate avoidance.

So there you have it; from exultant appointment to humiliating resignation in just a few easy to follow pages. But take heart; as we said in our very first chapter, ministerial office remains one of the greatest opportunities that any democratic system can bestow and one that offers the real possibility of improving the lives of, literally, millions of people. If you are willing to work hard and with determination, the chances that you will make a success of being a minister are really quite high. And, just perhaps, if you give some thought to some of the handy hints in the preceding pages, a little higher still.

# CHAPTER 10

# CIVIL SERVANTS

*It is not easy nowadays to remember anything so contrary to all appearance as that officials are the servants of the public; and the official must try not to foster the illusion that it is the other way round.*

SIR ERNEST GOWERS (1880–1966), *PLAIN WORDS*

AND THEN THERE'S THE CIVIL service. From the moment you become a minister, your relationships with your civil servants – your 'officials' to use that very strange term so beloved of Whitehall – will, as we have noted already, form a central part of your working life for one very good reason – your effectiveness as a minister will largely be determined by the quality and nature of these working relationships.

From that very first day, once you have met your new

private office team and very shortly afterwards the Permanent Secretary, your very own 'Sir Humphrey' or his female counterpart, there will be a steady stream of knocks on your door from the officials – most of whom will be complete strangers to you – who will be working on all of the areas covered by your portfolio. There will be the inevitable briefing pack on your new desk, bringing you up to date with current issues within your responsibilities and mapping out the areas where you will be required to make early decisions. You are bound to feel a mix of excitement and terror at what lies in front of you. But you can be sure of one thing right from the beginning – that the wheels of the machine will already be turning. Unbeknown to you, your private office will be rapidly filling up your diary with a series of briefing meetings between you and your key officials so that they can begin to get you familiar with your brief and, in return, understand what it is you want to do.

As a newly appointed minister you therefore need to think very hard about these first contacts with officialdom and what impression you want to make. From now on everything you say and do will be important to them. Your thoughts on any of the subjects you have responsibility for will be meticulously recorded and be the subject of extensive analysis within your department. This will almost certainly come as a surprise. Up until now, as a backbencher, few people, other than a handful of local journalists (if that), have probably paid any serious attention to anything you have said. All of this is about to change.

You naturally want your officials to regard you as a bright and intelligent person with a sense of purpose and direction. In practice that may or may not be the case; try asking your husband, wife, partner or kids what they think. But whatever they say is no reason not to try. Even if you are not yet clear about what it is you actually want to do, appearances nevertheless count for a great deal. So here are some tips to get you started.

First, put away the idea you may have picked up either in opposition or through the media that civil servants are all closet supporters of your political opponents and will want to frustrate you at every turn. Save in the very exceptional case it simply isn't true. In any event, paranoia is not an attractive trait and is unlikely to make a great start to your ministerial career. What is almost certainly true is that these very same officials helped your opponents devise and put into operation the very policies that you fought tooth and nail to stop – the very ones you described as a dog's breakfast. But that was then. Now, however surprising it may seem, they are ready to help you with your own plans.

Your officials will not expect you necessarily to know anything very much at the outset about your portfolio, indeed they will be a bit alarmed if you do, but they will expect you to be able to make decisions. This, as we have already noted, is, after all, what you are in the department to do. The system will fall down around your ears if you can't do this, or want endless extensions of time or more options before you make up your mind. It is always a good idea to have options, but one of them has to be selected as the way forward. The submissions – another strange Whitehall word – which you will begin receiving from officials almost straightaway are designed to frame the issues and extract these decisions from you.

From your perspective, you need to decide which of these decisions really have to be taken, or which you absolutely want to take, and which you may want to defer until you have a better sense of what you're about. Being able to ask your officials the right questions will undoubtedly help you make a start in the right direction. And you will almost certainly not want to take these early decisions – or at least the important ones – on the strength of these written submissions alone. Getting everyone around the table and talking the issues through is likely to be time well spent. And that means listening as well as speaking. The ability to listen to the advice you are getting from your officials is of first-order importance to you as a minister. But at the same time, and while you will want to canvass opinion from all of your advisers, remember always that the decision-making process within your department is not a democracy. There is only one person in the room who gets a vote on what to do – and that's you.

But even then, of course, getting decisions right isn't always easy. And – to labour a point we have made already – you are much less likely to do so if the civil servants round your table won't tell it to you as they really believe it to be. So our second key tip is to try to establish an open and confident relationship with them. Not only are you the only person who can do this but if you get it right it will stand you in good stead for as long as you remain in the department. Sadly, the contrary is also true.

So, you need early on to set the tone for the way you want your officials to behave towards you. Your private office, of which much more later, can help get things moving in the right direction. This small group of generally quite young civil servants will help connect you to the department and will also be the conduit through which your views, requests and concerns will be communicated back to officials. They will also have a unique insight into the work of other officials in the department and can provide you with both a useful commentary on what is really going on as well as a candid view on the advice you are receiving from officials. Not for nothing have private offices been called the league of double agents. It is therefore important, first and foremost, for you to have absolute confidence in this team of people. Let them and, through them, the wider department know how you like to work but, above all, satisfy yourself that you have the right people in the key positions in your private office – people who can add real value and extra insight to the official advice you are receiving in submissions. They are not there to act as postmasters and postmistresses. If you have any doubts it is far better to let your Permanent Secretary know straightaway. As we stress at greater length in our later chapter you need to have a private office team in which you can absolutely trust, not least as these will be some of the very few jobs over which you will get to express a very direct preference for who you wish to work with.

Your private office will also manage your diary. It is hard to exaggerate the almost transcendental importance of the ministerial diary. Everyone in the department will want to have access to it. So will many organisations and individuals outside the department. It has to be guarded carefully otherwise your job will become impossible. It is a document which will quickly take over your life unless you are prepared to exercise very clear control over what you want to do with it and with your time. However angelic a person you are, you are more likely to end up blowing your fuse over your diary than probably anything else, not least as it is usually assumed that a minister can work 24/7 for as long as your department deems it necessary. It will also be assumed that ministers have no bodily functions of any kind that need to be accommodated, so they never need to eat, relax, or even use the toilet. Ministerial time – your time – is a precious commodity and needs to be strategically managed. So the third key tip is that you have to be the one to determine how that time is spent. You are the one who decides what does or does not go into the diary and no one else.

Tip number four concerns style and behaviours. Although you now have a great deal of power over your officials, how you choose to exercise this authority will determine the sort of relationship you are going to have with them and how effectively they will work with you. As we noted earlier, remember that officials have seen it all before. The minister who tears up submissions in front of their hapless author. The screamer and shouter. The door slammer and paper weight chucker – incidentally you're in real trouble if the paperweight ends up accidentally smashing the PC; try keeping that out of the papers – the civil service has endured and survived it all. So keep one thing in your mind. Rule by terror is neither a sustainable nor a very intelligent way to work with people, especially when you will necessarily have to rely heavily on their professional skills and capabilities when things get tricky – as they most certainly will from time to time. Genuine authority and respect within your department will come not from the crude abuse of power but from its calm and measured exercise. Humility rather than hubris will take you a long way further. So will the occasional smile and 'thank you'. The more your officials feel valued, the more value they in turn will give you. That doesn't mean, as we have said, putting up with the shoddy or second rate; indeed you should make your standards and expectations very clear.

But it does mean behaving like a human being, not a latter-day Attila the Hun.

In particular, never forget that being a minister implies a two-way contract. Forget all the caricatures about people who don't know what it is to do a proper day's work. As you will discover, when the going gets tough your officials will be there night and day at your behest. They will work incredibly long hours to do the things you have asked them to do. In return, you owe some obligations to them, perhaps the most important of which is your duty to engage with them and be ready to make the necessary decisions. To do this you need to have read, digested and understood the material that has been prepared for you, and be in a position to communicate your views upon it. It is always tempting, particularly late at night when you are exhausted, to think you can bluff your way through, rather than read the papers for the next day's meetings. And once in a while you can; no one is paying you to be superhuman after all. But the wheels will come off very quickly if you try to avoid doing the work on a routine basis.

Tip number five is to understand the role of your civil servants in advising you about your dealings with other government departments. A lot of your time as a minister will be spent sitting on Cabinet sub-committees and, as if by magic, you will find briefs prepared by your officials appearing in your ministerial box in advance of each of these meetings. These are amongst the more important meetings you will be involved in. This is where the hard-wiring of joined-up government policy making takes place. But there is an obvious danger here – it is all too easy to become introspective and immersed in the internal world of your own department. Your officials will often have a good idea of where other departments are coming from and they can be very useful allies in helping you to broker deals and find ways forward. But they are not immune from pursuing what they perceive to be their own department's interests, which may or may not reflect yours or your party's. So make sure that your private office and officials are clear about where you stand on these cross-governmental questions. It is one of your most important jobs to manage the cross-Whitehall politics of policy making – not something you can or should delegate to your officials. Avoid at all costs turning up at these committee meetings and finding yourself reading out a dreary departmental brief which does not reflect your own view.

Finally, tip number six, don't be afraid of voicing concern if you don't think that your key officials are on top of things and that policy is not being moved forward in the way you want. It is the responsibility of the Permanent Secretary to ensure that your policy is being properly implemented and therefore you need to be able at all times to both voice your concerns about what is happening and expect remedial action where things are not going well. Hopefully it won't all be one-way traffic. Heaping praise on those who are doing their job well should also be seen as part of your job as a minister. Recognition for a job well done can go a very long way.

So there you have it, half a dozen tips for getting the best out of your civil servants. But of course one key issue is when and how often to look beyond your civil servants for advice. Ministers can only be effective instruments for change if the processes of policy making, policy implementation and risk management are all properly drawn together. Your officials are a key element of that and the better you can work with them, the more you will get from them. But, as we have discussed already, it is highly likely that on some issues you may well want to go outside the department altogether and seek the advice of others. This is a perfectly sensible thing to do and it can help you break the mould of settled opinion particularly where you feel that the perceived wisdom or status quo within the department has become too fixed or introverted for your own liking.

But a few words of advice about going down this path, in addition to those we have already set out in our chapter on analysis and experts. First, don't do it in secret. You have an absolute right to seek external advice on almost anything but what won't help is to seek it in a hole-in-the-corner way. Secondly, while you will obviously want to take some soundings about who might be suitable, it is essential for you to meet the person or people you are thinking about asking to undertake this work on your behalf so you can fully discuss the whole project with them. You must be able to have absolute confidence in them. Third, make sure you agree clear terms of reference for the project. This might seem straightforward enough but the boundaries set by these terms of reference will be rigidly patrolled by officials so it will be important from your perspective to establish the clearest possible remit to prevent the exercise from descending into a bureaucratic quagmire. Moreover, it is probable that there will be some ruffled feathers amongst your officials about your decision to go outside the department for advice so it is advisable to counter this quickly and decisively right from the beginning. This is something on which you need and have a right to expect support from your Permanent Secretary, so make sure you have fully involved your most senior adviser in your thinking. Finally, and of critical importance, make sure you and your Permanent Secretary unearth any possible conflicts of interest before going down this road; few things can be as damaging to a minister's reputation as to find out only after the event that the person you have just appointed to review your department's policy on procurement turns out to have a large financial interest in a major outsourcer or is being pursued by HMRC for several millions in unpaid tax.

In the end understanding the nature of your relationship with your civil servants is key. Many ministers will find policy making the most satisfying part of their job. But the job of a minister does not come to an end on the day that policy announcements are made. Funnily enough, White Papers do not implement themselves and legislation usually represents the beginning of any change process rather than its conclusion. One thing should be clear; policy making itself can readily be undermined by poor implementation, ineffective communication and inadequate risk assessment. As a minister, it is ultimately your job – not your officials' – to manage these hazards to the policy agenda you are pursuing. Your role in the department is to provide strategic vision and to manage the risk of policy failure and the resultant reputational damage to you personally and to the government in which you serve. Here lies perhaps the most intriguing dimension to ministerial life – the people who will work with you on all of these huge areas of consequence to you as a minister and on which so much will depend have not been chosen by you and you will have no line management responsibility for them of any kind. Your Permanent Secretary has this ultimate authority over the people you work with, not you. Your task is to craft a set of effective working relationships with officials, not to be their CEO. And, truly amazing this, you may end up liking rather a lot of them.

CHAPTER 11

# THE TOP TEAM

*In governments there must be both shepherds and butchers.*

VOLTAIRE (1694–1778)

ALL ORGANISATIONS HAVE HIERARCHIES AND yours is no exception. You may not have given a lot of thought to your department's top team but you probably should, not least because who they are, and how well they do their jobs, is a far more crucial determinant of your success than you might imagine. Some of them you will, of course, know very well. For better or worse you can't avoid the Permanent Secretary, about whom you may already have read our advice earlier in this volume. You will almost certainly know or get to know the director generals who head your department's policy areas pretty well too. But can you even name the HR director, the department's senior lawyer and the chief information officer without getting your private office to remind you? And yet they control some of your department's most important assets, indeed almost its only ones unless you have been unfortunate enough to inherit some ghastly holding in a long-forgotten company bailed out years back by one of your predecessors.

There was a time not all that many years back when departments did not have top teams in any sense that a private sector company would have recognised. To the extent that somebody had to do 'management' – not a word of which an old style mandarin would have had much understanding – it was left to those in the department thought not quite up to the job of doing 'policy', which was the only thing that really mattered. Thankfully, to a much greater extent than some commentators have given credit for, those days have very largely gone. Indeed it would probably surprise you to know just how much time your senior officials – including the policy ones – now spend on both management and its even more elusive cousin 'leadership'. Which is why you need to take this seriously too.

Now there is a substantial tome to be written about the extent to which ministers should be held accountable for all of the actions of their departments and about whether a sensible dividing line can be drawn between ministerial and civil service responsibilities. As already noted, we venture some thoughts on this ourselves in Part II of this volume. But what is clear is that no minister in charge of a department can simply regard everything other than policy and politics as somebody else's responsibility and nothing to do with them. On the day when all hell breaks loose and no one from Land's End to John O'Groats has been paid their benefits because of a massive computer failure, try telling the House that it's really none of your business. You will soon have the great pleasure of repeating your protestations from the backbenches.

On the other hand, about the worst thing you can do is to try and micro-manage your department. You certainly don't have the time and you very probably don't have the skills. So what is it you can and should do? Five things.

First, make time to meet your top team regularly. That is in addition to chairing your departmental board, which is a necessary but not sufficient involvement not least because most of the top team are not members of the board. Tell them your priorities and share your concerns honestly and openly. Only if your senior officials know what's on your mind and what's really worrying you can they try to do something to help. In return invite them to tell you what's top of their agenda and on their worry list. You may well be surprised about some of their issues and you may find that there is something you can do to help. But even if you can't you will gain their respect simply by asking and showing interest.

Secondly, meet reasonably often – say every six months as a minimum – with each of the top team members who you don't meet regularly as part of day-to-day business. That's likely to mean, principally, the heads of the support services such as HR and IT. Finance is every bit as important, of course, but you ought to have lots of contact with the Finance director anyway. Make clear in advance through your private office that the meetings are not going to be some kind of modern-day Spanish inquisition and that you don't want a long paper in advance – or indeed any paper lest you end up with a long one anyway – but that you simply want a chance to chat. You may well have a couple of things on your mind that you want to raise – and you certainly shouldn't hold back on raising areas about which you do have real concerns or worries – but, if not, your Private Secretary will undoubtedly give you a few thoughts, some of which may even be printable. Again the objective is simply that you both end up better informed.

With the same aim in mind also meet regularly with the key 'deliverers' in the department; i.e. the people – whatever their formal job title or position in the hierarchy – who head up the parts of the organisation responsible for putting your policies – and the department's day-to-day business – into practice. It has become part of the accepted political narrative that just as all politicians are corrupt, venal and self-seeking, so all bureaucrats are incapable of delivering the proverbial entertainment in a brewery. One former senior civil servant who swapped a very senior delivery role in government for an equally senior one in the third sector speaks of his amazement that the same Select Committee which had previously regarded him as scarcely worth the time of day now hung on his every word in explaining the challenges of delivery. The truth is that you almost certainly have some very able and experienced managers in your organisation whose advice not on what to do, but rather on how to do it if you want the policy to succeed, will be well worth listening to.

Thirdly, encourage each of your junior ministers to involve themselves equally in some aspect of the department's management. Now this can be tricky. You absolutely do not want a Rottweiler-style junior minister thinking that he or she has your personal fiat to overturn every decision your HR director or chief information officer takes. That is likely to end very quickly in tears and in one of those visits from the Permanent Secretary that you would far rather do without. But, at the other end of the spectrum, having one of your junior ministers genuinely interested in each of the department's key support services and willing to spend some of their time, constructively, in getting to know the issues and the people in a way you can never hope to do is likely to do only good. If this appeals talk through with your Permanent Secretary which ministers might cover which areas; that way if you have ended up with a Rottweiler – despite the Prime Minister having assured you that they would be a delightful colleague to work with – you can at least ensure that they are put to work on the department's most obscure and intractable policy problem. You never know, they might just solve it!

Fourthly, spend some serious time, reasonably regularly, with your department's non-executive directors including, but not exclusively, the lead non-executive for the department. The experience of having non-executive directors on the boards of government departments has been a somewhat chequered one and is still evolving. The direct parallel with the role of a non-executive on the board of a PLC just doesn't work. The legal and regulatory environment is entirely different and it is inconceivable that the non-executives on the board of a government department could in the end impose their will on the department in the way that they can, in extremis, in a public company. But, that said, there are parallels. The best non-executives on a departmental board will have an almost unique vantage point from which to assess the strengths and weaknesses not only of the department as a whole but also of its key leaders. They will be able to bring an experienced external perspective to what can sometimes still feel like a closed and semi-secretive world. They will have a sense of what can and can't be delivered brought not from reading endless submissions but from their own experience of the art of the possible.

So make time to meet and get to know them, not just in the formal and structured setting of the departmental board itself, but more informally either as a group or in one-to-ones. Be prepared to be open and to chew the fat. Let them know of your concerns and frustrations if you have them but also ask them to tell you honestly where they think the department is doing well and badly. If you feel able to, ask them – particularly your lead non-exec – to tell you where they think that you and your ministers may be hindering not helping. You may be surprised at how frank they are willing to be and how useful you may find it.

Finally, and coming back to your own most senior civil servants, recognise that just as you need your top team's support if you are going to achieve your objectives, they need yours if they are going to manage the department effectively. There is very little to be gained by setting yourself up in opposition to your top team and a great deal to be gained by not doing so. And – controversial this – think very long and hard before you lay into your department publicly, however strong the temptation. Telling Parliament that your department is not fit for purpose will undoubtedly get you the headlines as the strong man or woman but it is likely to leave a legacy of bitterness and distrust which you will never, ever outlive. Where your department has screwed up badly – and at some point in your time in office it probably will – you will in the end gain far more credit both inside and outside the department both by taking responsibility yourself, rather than by heaping it on to others, however well justified that might be, and by engaging in a serious, not headline-seeking, examination of what went wrong, why it went wrong and how best to reduce the chances of similar failures happening in the future.

So that's it for this chapter. Not one of the most exciting in the book. But then some of government isn't!

CHAPTER 12

# THE PRIVATE OFFICE

*The relations between a Minister and his Secretary are, or at least should be, among the finest that can subsist between two individuals. Except the married state, there is none in which so great a confidence is involved, in which more forbearance ought to be exercised, or more sympathy ought to exist.*

BENJAMIN DISRAELI (1804–1881)

THERE IS ONE COMMON FACTOR that lies behind all successful ministers. To be a successful minister you need to have a good private office. It is as basic as that. Life in Whitehall will be much harder without one. So this chapter is, unashamedly, written by the former minister amongst the two of us. But it contains nothing with which the former mandarin would disagree.

Let me first of all define my terms. By 'success' I mean your policies are well formulated and well executed, allowing you to focus on communicating your vision and strategy. By 'good' I mean your private office staff are able to provide effective support to you in spotting problems and difficulties that lie in your path to success and helping you to overcome them. So it will be of first-order importance to you to ensure you have the right team working in your private office.

The good news is that as a Secretary of State you should be in a position to pick the brightest and best of your younger officials to work in the private office. And usually there will be no shortage of good people who will want to work with the Secretary of State. If there is, it is probably personal. They will have heard the stories about how difficult you are to work for and how undervalued you make people feel, which is something for you to reflect on long and hard. But for a young and ambitious civil servant there are few more exciting places to be in a department. The private office sits right at the heart of things and the Secretary of State's private office is right at the top of the tree. It will have its eyes and ears on everything that is happening in the department, will communicate your instructions to the department and will be privy to the highest levels of decision-making across Whitehall. These young officials will work unbelievable hours alongside you and your Spads, and will be at your side for most of the time you are Secretary of State. You will come to rely heavily on them so it is right that you give very careful thought to who you want to be in the team.

The most important person in the private office will be the Principal Private Secretary – known to the entire department as the PPS. He or she will have the responsibility not just for your office but for all of the other ministerial private offices in your department and probably the Permanent Secretary's office as well. They will also manage your relations with the private offices of your Cabinet colleagues and No. 10, as well as providing vital feedback and intelligence to senior officials, including the Permanent Secretary, right across the department. The best act almost as the conductor in an orchestra – keeping people together and ensuring they come in at the right time with the right notes.

The skills a good Private Secretary needs to have are instinctive and personal rather than purely intellectual. And neither is an interest in politics a necessary qualification. Politics is your responsibility not that of your officials. But it is not just policy knowledge that makes for a good Private Secretary, important though this is. Of course you will want the Private Secretaries in your office – and especially your PPS – to have a good background in the subject areas they are responsible for, but it is the ability to manage relationships that is perhaps the most important attribute. In the private office, EI is just as important as IQ. Obviously the Private Secretary needs to work well with you as the Secretary of State but they need to be able to get the best out of others too. These are the skills you should be on the lookout for and regard as gold dust when you find them.

But this is only the beginning of what makes for an effective private office, because even the brightest junior officials will find it hard to add value in a system that still venerates seniority and hierarchy unless they are empowered by you to do so. Only you can do this which is why you need to be clear about the way you want to work with your private office.

First and foremost, you need to set the tone for how you

want your private office to work. If you are going to get the most from your private office your team need to feel confident enough to tell you when problems are developing. And remember that it's all very well saying that in theory. If on the day that one of your Private Secretaries comes in to tell you that officials are really unhappy with one of your decisions and suggests that you might just want to think again you bawl them out with a ferocity which leaves even the tea lady running for cover, don't be surprised if you never get such early warnings again.

You need in the same way to encourage your office to add their own commentary and thoughts on the advice you are receiving from officials. But if they are going to do these vital tasks well, then they in turn need to understand what it is you are trying to do. They must know your mind and, unless they are clairvoyant, you will need to sit down and talk to them about where you want things to go. So it is important that you make time for this to happen. At the same time your private office need to know that you absolutely don't want them looking serially askance at the rest of the department. The risk of having some very bright young people in your office is that they can tend to think that they know better than many of the officials they're dealing with. You absolutely want their energy and drive; but you don't want them standing between you and officials who may be less exciting but who have years of genuine expertise and experience to offer.

You must also be clear with your PPS about your red boxes and how you want your work load to be managed. I waited with growing excitement on my first day of office to see what would be in my evening red box. What a disappointment. Far from it being full of fascinating and secret things, it turned out to be full of a hundred humdrum things I could and should have done during the day. Staying up every evening until the early hours won't make you a good minister – it will just make you a tired and exhausted one.

The relationship between your Spads and the private office is another key issue to manage. Your Spads need to be able to work closely with your private office, to see whatever they want to see and to be fully involved in your work. But they are not there to tell your private office what to do. Set out the ground rules you expect with both your Spads and your private office right from the beginning and make sure they are stuck to. At the end of the day these relationships are your responsibility to oversee. If you allow effort to be devoured in pointless arguments and turf wars it will simply drain the energy and effectiveness of the whole operation.

And be very clear about one thing. Your Private Secretaries are not there to be your cheerleaders. And they are not part of your party political support team either, however close you might get to them as colleagues. Private offices can provide something much more important than such support. The best private offices should be able to provide engaged objectivity, a sound source of additional advice and pointers to you so that you can make the right decisions.

At a more detailed level one of the most important tasks of the private office is to take a minute of every meeting in which you are present, to record every decision you make and the reasons why you have come to this decision. These notes will form part of the all-important audit trail surrounding every action you take as a Secretary of State. They will be circulated across your department and to other interested departments across Whitehall. They are incredibly important documents. Your officials will take their cue from these notes and take forward measures to give effect to your wishes. They are the Whitehall equivalent of the Tablets of Stone. So it is entirely proper and reasonable for you to see these minutes before they are circulated. For all of the really important decisions you make it is a good idea to sign these off yourself so there is no ambiguity about what it is you want your officials to do in your name. Satisfy yourself that everyone has understood what was in your mind at the time. This is the best way to avoid any possible delays and misunderstandings in the future.

Remember, finally, one other thing. The flip side of your private office working under incredible pressure for all the hours that God sends is that sometimes they'll make mistakes and get things wrong. And sometimes embarrassingly so, as when they manage to send the note of the meeting with the CBI to the TUC and vice-versa. When that happens you don't have to be thrilled. But you do need to remember the hundreds of things they've got right for you over the past eighty-hour week before launching into the rant from hell.

The ministerial corridor in your department will always be a busy place with endless comings and goings, but the prevailing aura in the private office should be that of calmness and resilience and this should emanate from the PPS downwards. I was fortunate in working with some truly outstanding Private Secretaries – people like Tony Sampson at Health, John Oliver at the DWP and Richard Abel at BIS (Business, Innovation and Skills) – who allowed me to focus my time and energy on the projects that mattered the most to me and who helped me to assemble some really gifted officials to work as part of my private office team. They could also cope with the inevitable moments of crisis – where I would sometimes think about kicking the cat – and instead continue to think about how the department could help provide ongoing support and a way forward. Very strong bonds can be forged under these conditions. When I think back to my time as a Secretary of State it is my private office that first springs to mind. The sense of a shared journey, of working together and a pride in the product we all tried to deliver. They will be the ones who will see you at your best – and also at your lowest when you are in trouble with No. 10, the media, the Chancellor or all three. If it is working as it should, your private office and your PPS in particular can help you survive all the trials and tribulations of holding high ministerial office. If it isn't, then the job can become almost impossible. Make sure that doesn't happen to you.

CHAPTER 13

# THE TREASURY

*Pennies do not come from heaven. They have to be earned here on earth.*

MARGARET THATCHER (1925–2013)

THERE ARE DEPARTMENTS, REALLY IMPORTANT departments; and then there's the Treasury.

The Chambers definition of the Treasury as 'a place where funds are kept and disbursed' gives you the basic idea. Though today 'borrowed and barricaded' may get slightly closer to the reality.

Whatever the theory, however, there is little that you will be able to do without the Treasury in support of you and little that you won't be able to achieve with it behind you – but that is easier said than done. The Treasury exists fundamentally to stop you from spending. It is the one real counterweight in the whole of government to all of those forces who want, in the immortal words of Viv Nicholson when she won the Pools in 1961, to spend, spend, spend. Indeed it is no accident that almost all the other departments in government are called 'the Spending Departments'.

Of course, you're probably already thinking that you're different. You're close to the Chancellor politically and you get on OK with the Chief Secretary. Or even if you're not you've been appointed by the Prime Minister and he's told you that you'll have his full support. And anyway all you want to do (well maybe just a bit more) is implement the manifesto.

Think again. Even if it's the copper-bottomed policy of the government, the Treasury are going to be institutionally sceptical. And if it's not they are almost certain to be downright hostile. Their view, even if they think that you should be doing it at all, is that it can be done for half the price or, even better, by someone else like the private sector who will do it more effectively anyway. And they tend to have history on their side. They've heard all the rhetoric, read all the spreadsheets and, like the bookies, seen all the horses that could never lose. They've been left, time and time again, with the consequences of the contracts that went wildly over budget, the pay deals that ended up costing twice what they were meant to and the sure-fire policy changes that led not to savings and happiness but to overspending and grief. And it's not, after all, as if their own handling of the economy has been one of untold joy. Black Wednesday, expenditure forecasts that turned out to be wildly wrong and banks which went bust in the night have left them even more scarred and sceptical than ever. So if you're going to really get the Treasury on side you're going to have to work pretty hard.

There is another route, of course, and that's to try and outflank them. If you really have got the Prime Minister on your side you might just – just – be able to get him or her to override them. But as high-risk strategies go, they don't get much higher than this. However much No. 10, or even the Prime Minister personally, want something, they are going to be loath to over-rule the Chancellor. There is simply no mileage in a Prime Minister and Chancellor being at daggers drawn, as recent history has shown. And even if you can get No. 10 to force the Treasury, despite all of the above, to cough up money for a particular programme over their dead body, you are likely to end up paying a very large price for a very long time. Like the elephant, the Treasury never forgets. Don't believe for a moment that we're all professional and we'll leave the past behind us. The Treasury will get its own back and you and your department will be the losers.

So how do you try to get the Treasury behind you? Trying to get genuine political agreement is a pretty obvious place to start. Invest time and effort – lots of it – in talking to the Chancellor and the Chief Secretary. Try to work out which one of them is the prime mover on each of the key issues you want to make progress on and then seek to persuade and explain, rather than browbeat and hector. And listen to what they say. They may just have a better idea anyway and, even if you're not convinced, there's almost always something you can compromise on. Treasury ministers are just like anyone else; they want to think they're making a difference.

Think very hard too about how you want to position your department in respect of the big set-piece spending reviews which will be an ever-present and recurring feature of your ministerial life. If there is one iron law of politics it is that the

Treasury will want to end up with your department spending lots less than you do. That will apply even if you're in one of the 'protected' departments like Health or Overseas Development. If you're in one of the 'also rans' you will face far greater pressure just to cut.

Now there is no single 'right' response to this. Much will depend on your own political position within the government and how much you believe that there is genuine scope to reduce your department's spending. You will almost certainly face huge pressures at times both from within the department and from the bodies it funds to dig in and fight your corner. Indeed your political machismo can all too easily come to be seen as inextricably linked to your willingness to stand up and be counted. The difficulty though is that in the end, taken across government as a whole, the Treasury is likely to have to prevail if overall levels of public expenditure are to be kept within acceptable limits and the confidence of the markets retained. So, while you will never want to be seen as a soft touch, and you need to recognise that there will almost certainly be some give in the Treasury's 'ask' of your department at least round the edges if you are prepared to argue, there may often be more mileage in being willing to 'settle' relatively early on – particularly if you can gain a few concessions that matter to you by doing so – than in fighting to the last breath in a battle that in the end you almost certainly can't win.

And remember also that, almost uniquely amongst finance ministries in the Western world, the UK Treasury is also an economic ministry. As such it will also have views – often very decided ones – about what constitutes good and bad spending. So, for example, from an economic perspective it will always prefer spending which promotes economic growth – infrastructure investment, spending to reduce welfare dependency and promote labour market growth and the like – over spending on what it sees simply as drains on public expenditure like benefits and defence. That helps explain why the Treasury's relationships with the MoD are so perennially bad – because the Treasury wants simply to reduce defence spending and can't see why we need more admirals than ships.

Of course if you've just been appointed to the MoD there's not a lot you can do to shift fundamentally such deeply held views. But the Treasury are also realists; they recognise that there are generally more votes for building frigates than for building prisons. And, for your part, there are ways of presenting and tailoring your spending plans that, even on stony ground like defence, will make them more attractive to the Treasury from an economic perspective.

Your special advisers matter too. If they have a good relationship with their Treasury opposite numbers it can be worth its weight in gold. If they're barely on speaking terms you're in deep trouble. Sometimes, as we have noted already, Spads can do the deals that no one else can. They generally have the licence – and even if they don't the really good ones will take it anyway – to think outside the box and come up with the trade-offs. Paradoxically that can also be a good route if personal relationships at the political level are bad; the best Spads won't want simply to continue the fight. They'll want to see if there is some kind of win/win to be had.

And don't forget your officials and their relationship with the Treasury either. It really matters. Remember that every time you meet a Treasury minister they, just like you, will have a brief from their officials. It's a brave Treasury minister who is going to over-rule them, not least because on all but the very biggest things on your agenda they're not going to have much of a clue what it's all about. They simply can't have given the vast waterfront they have to cover. So they're going to be almost wholly dependent on their officials to tell them what the issue is about and 95 per cent of the time they're going to go with their advice as to the line they should take.

But remember their officials are also dependent on your officials. Treasury civil servants are good. Man for man, and woman for woman, probably the best in Whitehall. But even they can't hope to understand a vast department like the DWP or the Ministry of Defence, let alone a very specialist one like International Development or Energy and Climate Change, in the way your own officials can. They depend absolutely on your officials for facts and information. And, if they respect your officials and their competence, they will pay a great deal more attention to what they say.

Now there are two schools of thought about this amongst ministers. Technically they are known as the 'tell them nothing' or the 'tell them everything' schools. Ministers who subscribe to the first tend to believe that the Treasury, given the chance, will turn every fact they are given against them or, worse, use the information to come up with alternative, and generally much less palatable, options. Ministers who subscribe to the second tend to believe that, in general, the Treasury are likely to come to a saner view if they are better informed than if they aren't and it will at least stop them from making it up for themselves.

The first view does have something going for it. There are times when it is probably better to hold some information back, particularly where the department itself is not yet clear what its own ministers want or when the Treasury are clearly determined to try and stop a policy at all costs. But in general it's a bad idea. The Treasury will in the end have to be given the facts and they have lots of well-honed defence mechanisms to prevent themselves from being bounced at the last moment. Keeping them in the dark, particularly when they know that is being done, will simply hack them off, generally to no good purpose. And it may well weaken the position of the department's own spending team in the Treasury – the people who are marking your department day in day out – who may well, unbeknown to you, actually be fighting your corner with others in the Treasury who are less well disposed to what you and your department want to do.

In practice, of course, there will be times when you will want your officials to tell the Treasury less, and times when you will want them to tell them more. But mostly the latter will get you the better result.

Talking of 'times', there are also two big, set-piece events every year – the Budget in the spring and the autumn statement (though in the finest Whitehall tradition the 'autumn' can slip to November if it appears expedient for it to do so) – when even the most fiscally conservative Chancellor wants to be able to announce something eye-catching and, if possible, actually popular. That is a great opportunity – particularly if your Spads get on with the Treasury Spads – to influence the agenda and get something you actually want slipped through. So begin to think a good few months out what that something might be and begin to lay the ground for it. And don't worry about the Chancellor taking the credit for it publicly; sooner or later if whatever it is works the credit will find its way back to you.

Finally, and all year round, never forget that your officials will be working day to day with the Treasury on a whole range of issues that you will hardly ever see; parliamentary estimates, contractual approvals, write-offs, accounting practices and much else besides. It may be tempting to believe that none of this matters much – though you'll end up having to know far more than you ever wanted to about it on the day it all goes pear-shaped – but it does. It is this kind of stuff which will either gain your department a reputation in the Treasury for being fundamentally competent or, alternatively, for not being able to run the proverbial whelk stall. If your department is in the latter category you and it are in deep trouble because it will colour the Treasury's view of everything you are trying to do. So talking to your Permanent Secretary and your Finance director about some of the more mundane things will be time well spent. And satisfying yourself, as far as you can, that your own officials know what they're about is pretty important too.

Love it or hate it the Treasury really matters. They can make you or break you. So don't under-invest in trying to build a relationship where, at the very least, they trust you and your department. There are few more important things if you really want to succeed.

CHAPTER 14

# SPENDING WATCHDOGS – THE NAO AND THE PAC

*While acknowledging the complexity of Operation 'Overlord', it is clear that there were a number of major weaknesses in its planning, execution and evaluation. Although the ultimate objective of the liberation of Europe was achieved, this was only at the cost of substantial failings in terms of missed deadlines, cost overruns and equipment shortfalls. In particular the value for money obtained was poor and the superficial nature of the post-invasion evaluation means that valuable lessons may have been missed in terms of future such operations.*

REPORT BY THE NATIONAL AUDIT OFFICE INTO THE D-DAY LANDINGS, MAY 1945

HOW MUCH YOU NEED WORRY about the implications for your department of the work of the National Audit Office – the NAO – and the Public Accounts Committee – the PAC – depends in part on the nature of your department. If it is a small, essentially policy department the work of the NAO and the PAC is likely to impact only to a relatively small degree on your priorities. If, on the other hand, you are heading a major delivery department, like the MoD or DWP, or a department at the heart of government like the Treasury or the Cabinet Office, then you are likely to find yourself having to react much more frequently to their findings. Either way the risks of not taking this seriously are real.

Now you can, of course, take the view that this is all fundamentally for the Permanent Secretary and not for you. Not only is it his or her responsibility to run the department effectively but it is also the case – blissfully – that unlike all other Committees of Parliament, the PAC is the one that will routinely call your Permanent Secretary to appear before it rather than you. So you will not have to spend hours mugging up on whichever obscure subject the NAO have decided to report on in advance of the PAC hearing into the issue. You can simply express vague sympathy to the Permanent Secretary that they have to go to yet another PAC hearing and then move on to the real business of the day.

But that would, almost certainly, be a mistake. It is indeed the case that if a PAC hearing goes badly it is the Permanent Secretary who is going to feel the hit much more directly than you. And it is equally true that most NAO reports and most PAC hearings – but beware the exceptions – get a few columns on the following day in the more serious newspapers but generally not much more. But that is to miss the point that what is really at stake at PAC hearings on your department is its reputation. That's why any Permanent Secretary worth their salt worries about this so much. If your department is routinely savaged over a long period – as, for example, the MoD has been – for managerial incompetence then it becomes much, much harder to gain agreement either within government or outside of it for the policies and changes that you yourself want to make. And, by definition, the converse is also true.

The even greater risk, as far as you are concerned, is where the NAO and the PAC get their teeth into a high-profile policy – such as NHS reform or Universal Credit – on which your own credibility is also riding. In practice, in such cases the supposed distinction between responsibility for the policy – the Secretary of State – and its implementation – the Permanent Secretary – very quickly breaks down because it's virtually impossible to tell whether things are going wrong as a result of an over-ambitious policy driven forward to an unrealistic timetable or a sensible, good-value policy derailed by incompetent delivery. In such cases it would be as well to recognise that you and your Permanent Secretary are the more likely to hang separately, the less you succeed in hanging together.

At this point – though it is not strictly part of this book's advice to you, so you can skip over the next few paragraphs if you want to – it is worth saying something about both the NAO and the PAC.

The NAO has existed in its present form since 1983 though its origins go back to at least the end of the eighteenth century. It exists to scrutinise expenditure on behalf of Parliament. In practice it has two main roles. First, it is the auditor of your department's accounts. In that sense – though the rules to which it operates are not completely identical – it plays fundamentally the same role in relation to your department that a company's auditors play in relation to a PLC. In particular it is required to give its opinion each year on whether your department's accounts give a 'true and fair' view of its financial position and on whether its expenditure has been in accordance with parliamentary or other authority; in essence whether it has been used for the purposes for which that money has been voted by Parliament.

Secondly, it carries out on behalf of the PAC each year a series of so called 'value for money' studies into specific aspects of departments' work, looking at whether the taxpayer has got value for money for their expenditure. Interestingly, in this second role, it is not allowed – supposedly at least – to question the underlying policy, which it is required to take as a given, but rather how that policy has been implemented in practice. Depending on the size and nature of your department it may carry out anywhere between one and up to ten such studies each year into aspects of your department's work. Not all of these studies lead to a PAC hearing but most do.

There is no doubt that, overall, the NAO is a force for good in our system of government as also is the PAC. Both have a track record over many years of rooting out managerial incompetence – and occasionally worse – in the higher echelons of government and the fact that they exist undoubtedly makes government more effective, and indeed more honest, than it might otherwise be. 'Could I defend this if I had to before the PAC?' is not merely a rhetorical question; it is one that most Permanent Secretaries find that they are often asking themselves when faced with a particularly challenging or difficult decision. If the answer is 'no' or 'only with difficulty' most will look instead for an alternative that they could defend with a completely clear conscience if called upon to do so. It is also undoubtedly the case that the work of the NAO and PAC over many years – by shining a powerful light on examples of administrative incompetence and failure – has drawn out valuable lessons in terms of what is likely to make for successful and unsuccessful delivery of major projects, particularly in the area of information technology. Moreover, at its simplest, the public are entitled to know how well or badly their taxes are being spent. The work of the NAO and PAC is one means by which they can do so.

So that's all alright then? Well only up to a point. For all this comes at a cost. There are two major charges to be laid against both the NAO and the PAC. The first is that they know the cost of everything and the value of nothing. The second is that they tend to make government particularly risk averse by placing powerful incentives within the system in favour of opting for the 'safe' solution over the potentially more beneficial but higher-risk option.

In relation to the first, the classic NAO value for money report – rather like the mythical example quoted at the beginning of this chapter – is so far into the trees that it can almost totally lose sight of the wood. A good example is the repeated NAO studies into fraud and error in the benefit system which are a regular feature of its work programme. Each takes as its starting point the very high levels of fraud and error in the benefit system – something around £3 billion a year – and castigates the departments concerned – primarily the DWP – for failing to reduce it through better procedures, more effective staff training, better recovery of overpayments and the like. The PAC – never knowingly averse to the attention-grabbing headline – adds to the mix by castigating the civil servants concerned as rogues, fools and knaves who, if only they were willing to put in the necessary effort, could and should sort all this out. The media then completes the production by calculating the number of additional teachers, hospitals or battleships (though the last of these are no longer as popular as they once were) that could be bought for £3 billion and pronouncing the outcome as a national scandal.

As a piece of theatre this is hard to beat. As a serious enquiry into why these levels of fraud and error exist and what could actually be done to reduce them it barely rises above the trivial. In particular it ignores the fundamental issue of the hideous complexity of the benefit system which has grown piecemeal over more than half a century to the point where there are now so many separate benefits, benefit rules and entitlement conditions that the system has simply gone beyond the point at which its beneficiaries have any chance of understanding it, let alone its staff of administering it. Against that background it is little short of a minor miracle that losses from fraud and error are only some 2 per cent of total expenditure. But that is a conclusion which would implicate not only those who administer the system but also those who have legislated for every piece of additional complexity over so many years. Far easier simply to blame the civil servants. Regrettably there are all too many other examples of where both the NAO and PAC duck the real issues in favour of the eye-catching condemnation.

The charge of incentivising government departments to be congenitally risk averse is, if anything, more serious. Not all of this is down to the NAO and PAC of course. The nature of government, and the traditional recruitment patterns into the civil service, tend not to breed many budding Richard

Bransons – and probably just as well. The private sector is inherently better suited to managing risk than the public sector, and more experienced at doing so. The belief – normal in the private sector – that part and parcel of running a business is that some products and services will inevitably fail is always going to be more difficult for the public and Parliament to accept when the failures end up costing the taxpayer, rather than the shareholder, money.

But that is not to say that all risk-taking in government is bad. On the contrary – while government can indeed be guilty of stumbling into hugely high-risk ventures which the private sector would rarely contemplate – without some genuine risk-taking there will, almost by definition, be no real progress or innovation in the business of government and in the delivery of its services to the public. Without innovation and risk there would be no online channels, no Oyster cards, no self-service job banks in Jobcentres and the like.

In an ideal world the NAO and the PAC would both be forces for more innovation and more well-judged risk. One former Permanent Secretary suggested that the PAC should hold to account those of his colleagues who could demonstrate no serious programme of innovation and change rather than those who could. In practice, however, both the NAO and the PAC exercise a highly chilling effect on risk and innovation. Having seen, or indeed personally experienced, the savagery or withering sarcasm of the PAC in particular when faced with a failed programme or project, it is little wonder that throughout government there is a tendency to play for safety and stick to the status quo. Few, if any, Permanent Secretaries have been hauled before the PAC for simply doing averagely well this year what they did averagely well last. And the more exaggerated the condemnation when things go wrong the less chance there will be of those within government who really do want to make it better, but who know that this can never be risk-free, being given the time and the space in which to innovate.

Is there any real chance of this changing? Depressingly, not much. Successive chairs and members of the PAC will, in the abstract, occasionally make speeches about their wish to incentivise good government. And once in a blue moon the committee will actually find something to praise. But the temptation to focus relentlessly on the failures, and to portray them in the most lurid of terms, proves in practice far too tempting. For its part the NAO will sometimes decry in private the way its reports are treated by the PAC but the truth is that they know which side their bread is buttered; the PAC expects them to serve up a regular diet of red meat, or at least red-faced Accounting Officers, into which it can sink its teeth, and in general they are only too happy to oblige. The contrast with departmental Select Committees in this respect is sometimes quite sharp. They vary considerably not least according to the quality of their chairs; but the better of them do seek to enquire in a more balanced way into the departments they shadow and they are more willing in general to give credit where they think it is due.

But enough already. This chapter is in danger of having gone from being advice to ministers to a therapy session for former Permanent Secretaries. As a minister what is it that you should actually do? Nothing too miraculous here. First, do recognise that, just as major parliamentary set pieces are high profile and stressful for you, so are PAC hearings for your Permanent Secretary. At the very least take the trouble to know when they are happening and make a point of asking afterwards how they have gone. If the Permanent Secretary has clearly done well at a very difficult hearing make a point of congratulating them. If not at least express some sympathy. That will probably be appreciated more than you might think.

Secondly, if you think that an NAO or PAC report really is being unfairly critical of your department be prepared to say so publicly. That may not, in truth, do much to shift the way the issue is reported but it will do wonders for the morale of your department. There is something of a tendency inside government to believe that challenging the conclusions of the PAC head-on is akin to challenging the referee, and equally unproductive. And it is almost certainly true that nothing your department says or does is likely to cause the PAC to think again. But where you and the Permanent Secretary genuinely believe that they have simply got it wrong, or are being grossly unfair, you probably owe it to the people at the receiving end of the criticism to say so.

And thirdly, particularly in those high-profile cases where the fire from the NAO and the PAC is particularly intense, resist the temptation, and the pressure that may come from some of those around you, to try to shift the blame, publicly or privately, on to your civil servants. Even if you think they deserve it, and they may do, there will be little to be gained even in the short term, and much to be lost particularly in the long term, from being seen to be taking cover behind your own troops in this regard.

More difficult, self-evidently, is where – while standing alongside your department publicly – privately you think the criticisms are justified and that the department should simply have done much better. In that case you need at the very least to do as much as you think necessary to satisfy yourself that the department, and indeed the Permanent Secretary, really have lifted up the drains and are taking action to put matters right. But even then you would probably do well to spare the abuse. The PAC will have handed out enough of that already.

CHAPTER 15

# PARLIAMENT

*You must build your House of Parliament upon the river so that the populace cannot exact their demands by sitting down around you.*

DUKE OF WELLINGTON (1769–1852)

IN OPPOSITION, AND AS A backbencher, the House of Commons will have been your main place of work. You will have spent much of each working day in and around the Houses of Parliament – which, as workplaces go, is one of the finest and most historic environments anyone can work in. You will probably have cut your teeth and earned your parliamentary spurs serving on a Select Committee or taking an interest in a specific area of policy through the work of an All-Party Parliamentary Group. And then of course there was the opportunity to participate in the regular duelling at Question Time every day of the week.

But Parliament is likely to have been more than just your place of work. It probably became your home from home. In opposition you are likely to have been spending between twelve and fifteen hours a day in and around the Commons. It is where you socialised with your colleagues, where you got to know and hopefully liked each other a little. It will have become a very big part of your life.

By the time you become a Secretary of State you should have had plenty of opportunity to feel comfortable in the Chamber, be capable of dealing with questions and debates, know how to conduct yourself in front of a Select Committee and how to make important statements on behalf of the government. So how is it that as a Secretary of State it risks becoming one of your biggest potential banana skins?

The answer is because it now matters much more. Being an effective parliamentary performer is one of the most important tests every minister must be able to pass. It is important – to inspire confidence – for your officials to know that they have a Secretary of State who can handle Parliament well. It is equally crucial – to protect your political reputation – for your parliamentary colleagues to believe that you are completely on top of your brief. And from your own point of view, no Cabinet minister wants to be labelled in the media as the 'weak link' in the ministerial chain, lined up to be demoted at the next reshuffle or booted out of the government altogether. Why then do so many senior ministers end up handling Parliament so badly?

It is probably best to begin at the beginning. When you become a minister it is very easy indeed to lose touch with the Commons. You get transported from the environment where you have spent most of your time to an altogether different world – your new department. Suddenly you are spending never-ending days buried in your new office or in meetings with your colleagues across Whitehall, deciding on policy, and with your diary absolutely bursting with an endless sequence of meetings and briefings. And if that's not enough you will also be travelling all over the country ('I fear, minister, that the Cement Manufacturers' Annual Dinner really is a must') and sometimes abroad on government business. In these heady times it is very easy to fall into the trap of regarding Parliament almost as a distraction – of much less importance than your ministerial ivory tower – and as something that simply imposes unwelcome extra pressure on to your diary.

If you fall into this trap you won't be the first and you won't be the last but it will be a fundamental error. If you doubt that, step out of your office and take another look at that long row of photographs of your predecessors. Ask yourself why so many vanished without trace and you will have your answer in some cases at least. Unless you want to find yourself written off by the backbenches as too grand to care you need to afford real priority to your relationship with Parliament, second only to your relationship with the Prime Minister.

There is another reason too why you should not take your eye off Parliament. There are clear signs now that the recent reforms in the House of Commons, for example the election of Select Committee chairs and the greater role given to backbenchers in deciding what business comes before the House, together with the new approach from the Speaker in bringing ministers to the House to answer urgent questions, are beginning to alter the balance of power between Parliament and the executive. For far too long the pendulum had been swinging in the wrong direction. The boot is now increasingly on the other foot.

There are two things that follow on from this.

First, to do your job in Parliament properly you need time in your diary to prepare yourself for questions, debates and Select Committee sessions. This is easier said than done given all the other calls on your time. So ensure that your private office and parliamentary branch in the department know to carve out enough time for you to go through the parliamentary business carefully. Be clear with them about the sort of briefing you require. As you prepare for Departmental Questions, for example, it is very easy to drown in a sea of briefings and, unless you instruct your officials otherwise, to find yourself submerged under enormous volumes of largely pointless Q&As which only make it harder for you to focus on the really important stuff. Many ministers, by contrast, find it helpful to have two or three key points to make in their follow-up answers – simple factual points that have the aim of undermining criticism of the government's policy. Of course even that may be of little assistance when the supplementary question travels well beyond any reasonable connection to the subject matter of the original ('The minister says he is in favour of reducing carbon emissions; would he like to tell my constituents therefore – who are frankly aghast – why he used his official car to attend the England versus Azerbaijan game at Wembley rather than using the Underground?').

Here you are on your own with no instruments to guide you other than your own instinct and judgement. In the Commons, when your briefing provides no clue as to what to say and you may not even have understood or heard the question, the tried and tested formula is simply to say how appalling the other party's record in government was and how you won't be taking any lectures from them on this or any other subject. In truth this is pretty thin gruel. It may get you a few limp cheers from the benches behind you (never to be dismissed entirely out of hand) but you need to be able to deal with specific policy issues affecting your department better than this. It is a tactic often regretted after the event. In this respect it's a pretty good rule of thumb to try and think how your answers will sound to people watching or listening to the parliamentary channel as they are probably the people most likely to vote. If you end up sounding just like all the other politicians who can't answer a question properly no one will be listening when you suddenly find yourself with something interesting to say. The simple motto therefore is 'be prepared'. Keep your briefing simple and manageable so you can focus on the important arguments you want to make. Know what you want to say. Rehearse your key lines – fluffing them will be embarrassing. Above all, try to answer the questions. Ignore the cynics. You may be surprised at just how much credit you get.

For debates, there is no rule book to follow. It really is a question of personal style. Some like to have a detailed speech to read out. Others prefer to have notes they can refer to. What is usually a recipe for a car crash is to have neither. The Commons can be a rumbustious and unforgiving place and your opponents will be doing all they can to put you off your stride. This is especially true of the winding-up speeches at the end of the debates. It is very easy in these circumstances to lose your train of thought altogether. Make sure you have the backup of a proper speaking note which can give you at least an outline of the main arguments you want to get across.

If you have something important to say for the record, then it is almost universally the case that you need to have your words clearly written down, so there is no mistake or ambiguity about what your policy is. Your opponents will thrive on ambiguity; the government will only be damaged by it.

Select Committees are no less of a challenge particularly now that they are beginning to develop some much sharper teeth. The recent reforms to the appointment of Select Committee chairs have made a marked impact on their independence and effectiveness and you need to regard an appearance before them as a major exercise requiring careful preparation. You need to be on top of both the strategy and the detail. And when it comes to the detail, there is nothing quite as impressive as a Secretary of State who goes before a Select Committee on their own, without the comfort and protection provided by the presence alongside them of senior officials in their department. Every member of the committee knows why these officials are present – they are there as bodyguards to shield you from having to know the detail. Only you can make the call on this. Officials can provide immensely valuable support which can ease the pressure on your preparation time. But, and it is a big but, you cannot pass on responsibility for all of the detail to others. You must have a solid grounding on the finances, the technology, and the implementation challenges that underpin your policy. Going to give evidence on your own is a clear sign to the committee (and the media) of your personal authority and grasp. But if you are going to do this, then you must have prepared properly.

If you are making a statement or answering an urgent question, then proper preparation is equally essential. Clear the diary and focus relentlessly on what you are going to say. You will have a draft from officials to consider but only you can judge the right tone to strike. You have to know your policy and your facts inside out. If you don't, it will be clear to everyone that you are not on top of things, which is never a good place to be. The late and much lamented Alan Clark could get away with almost never knowing the detail – one of us was in the House on the famous occasion when, as an employment minister arguing against the closed shop, he was unable to say what the initials GMBATU stood for, despite having spent the previous ten minutes lambasting the union for its actions – but he was a one-off and the exception that proves the rule. Very few ministers are able to turn a lack of knowledge into a virtue.

Statements are at least brief events but by definition they are particularly important occasions when the eyes of the media and your colleagues will be upon you. It is your opportunity to shine and to impress the House with your grasp of both the policy and the detail. In that context always give the opposition as much advance notice of your statement as possible. This is not just an appropriate courtesy. It is also a discipline which can avoid the last-minute rush to finalise what it is you are actually going to say, which is never the best way to go into the Chamber.

Second, and more generally, remember always that there is no substitute for ensuring that you meet regularly with your own parliamentary colleagues. Don't allow yourself to get isolated from them. When the going gets rough these are the people who can help you through a crisis in one piece. Your junior ministers and Parliamentary Private Secretary can help maintain communication between you and your backbenchers but there is nothing like speaking personally to the Secretary of State. Always find time in your diary or in the Lobby for colleagues who want to discuss their genuine concerns. It might just be a local constituency matter or they may want to discuss the policy you are pursuing in your department. The key thing is that they want to feel that they matter enough to be listened to. The importance of this cannot be underestimated. The same courtesies should be extended to opposition Members – you are, after all, accountable to the whole House and not just to your own side – although it is striking how rarely ministers are ever approached by opposition MPs in this way.

Last, but not least, your departmental Whip should be your other key channel of communication with the backbenches. If you hold regular ministerial team meetings – and if you don't, you should – it is enormously helpful to have your Whip in attendance to brief you and your ministers about the parliamentary mood as it affects your department. Your Whip is a key part of your parliamentary radar which you need to keep switched on. As a Secretary of State you should also be having regular chats with the Chief Whip to keep up to date with the wider agenda across government (and with the gossip, which is always much more fun).

Enough; you get the drift. Parliament – not Sky News – is where you will ultimately prove yourself to be a good minister. Take it seriously. It will never be wasted effort.

## CHAPTER 16

# THE EU

*I am sick of all this horrid business of politics, and Europe in general, and I think you will hear of me going with the children to live in Australia, and to think of Europe as the moon!*

QUEEN VICTORIA (1819–1901) IN A LETTER TO THE PRINCESS ROYAL, 1859

EUROPE. NOT ONLY ARE YOU having to deal with Westminster, Whitehall and Wakefield – or wherever your constituency is – as the Secretary of State you are going to have to deal with Brussels and Strasbourg as well; the dreaded EU.

Now you may be one of those rare ministers who feel deeply at home in the European corridors of power; for whom the Berlaymont and the Charlemagne[1] are as much home ground

1 Two of the key EU buildings in Brussels.

as the Commons Tea Room and your constituency office. You spent much of your childhood in France so your French is probably better than your English; you started your working life in either the Diplomatic Service or the Banque de Paris; and you think *Le Monde* is far better written than *The Times*. Indeed your partner, who you met on that weekend in Geneva which thankfully both of you have now largely forgotten, speaks fluent Italian too, which comes in very handy on your annual holiday in Tuscany.

Or much more likely you're not. You are likely, of course, to have had to make quite a few trips to the Fisheries Council when you were a junior minister in Defra or to one of those informal Social Affairs Councils when you were in DWP (you still wince at the memory of the one where you had rather too much ouzo at the meeting in Kos and were somewhat the worse for wear on the plane home). But, apart from reading out some of the world's most tedious speeches written for you by your officials and then having to listen to even more tedious ones being translated from the original German, none of this has left you with either much enthusiasm for the European ideal or any real understanding of how the actual business gets done, which always seemed to have been largely stitched up by the diplomats in Brussels before a single minister entered the room. So to say that you are keen to pick up the EU reins again as Secretary of State is something of an exaggeration.

There are reasons, of course, why you may nevertheless want to take a different view. If you are either a committed Europhile or a committed Eurosceptic then regular appearances on the Euro stage will undoubtedly give you a platform for getting more air time for your views. And if your department is one of those like Defra, where at least as much of what really matters gets decided in Brussels as in Westminster, then you probably have no alternative but to pitch in personally in quite a big way. But if you're not in one of these categories then the first question to decide is how much of your own time you actually want to spend on Europe.

If the answer is somewhere between not very much and as little as possible then it is perfectly feasible to leave almost all of the department's EU business to one or more of your junior ministers. And that may make even more sense if one of them happens to be fluent in French or another major EU language. You will still need, of course, to be deeply sympathetic to their tales of distress at having been delayed for three hours on Eurostar on their way back from the latest council and to evince some interest in their account of how, against all the odds, they were able to form a blocking minority with the Poles and the Maltese to stop the latest health and safety directive from going through. But for the most part you can simply get on with what you think you really have to do.

Be aware, though, that there are big risks in this approach as well as benefits. The first is that you and your department simply miss out on the potential benefits, as well as risks, that the EU can bring. Forget for a moment all the stories about straight bananas and overpaid Eurocrats so beloved of some sections of the media. The fact is that the EU not only now disposes of many hundreds of millions of Euros; it also sets the terms of the debate across a huge range of issues. UKIP may well be exaggerating substantially when they allege that three quarters of our laws are now 'made in Brussels'. But what is undoubtedly true is that there are big areas of public policy where the UK is simply not able to act unilaterally. And even where it is not directly legislating, the EU's influence – for better and worse – can be considerable. By leaving all this to your junior ministers you risk you and your department simply becoming increasingly out of touch with developments across Europe. While sitting next to the Spanish Health Minister at the dinner before the council meeting may not be your idea of an ideal evening it may be time well spent if you come away with a better sense of where Spain is coming from on the key 'dossiers' affecting your department and of whether you have a potential ally personally or politically.

The second risk is when you are faced with a piece of EU business or decision-making which directly impacts or threatens a key part of your own department's work or, even worse, which is suddenly all over the tabloids ('Now they want to ban our Christmas puds; EU meddlers say sultanas are a health risk'). On that day all of those slightly tedious meetings in Brussels or Strasbourg may come into their own if they mean that the relevant EU Commissioner and some of the key MEPs in the Parliament know you well enough to be willing to lift a finger to help. And that dinner with the Spanish Health Minister may also turn out to have been worth its weight in gold if she is willing to add her voice to yours in the corridors that matter. In other words if you put in next to no time getting to know the key European decision-makers don't be that surprised if they're mysteriously unavailable to take your call on the day you really do need to talk to them.

The truth is that, as in most things, there is a balance to be struck. Unless you really are a Euro enthusiast, or what the EU is doing is at the very heart of your department, you will probably neither want, nor be able, to attend every EU council or European Parliament meeting, meet every one of your EU counterparts (try just naming all the other twenty-seven countries for a start), learn French, German or Spanish, or pay bilateral visits to all the key capitals. A lot of this, perforce, is going to have to fall on the shoulders of your junior ministers and senior officials. But you probably want to do at least enough yourself to be recognised as a serious player. That is likely in the end to pay serious dividends. And that means not just being prepared to put in a shift or three personally in Brussels or Strasbourg and, in particular, meeting fairly regularly with the EU Commissioner or Commissioners whose brief covers your department's work. It also means having a sufficient understanding of the key dossiers which affect the work of your department to know what the UK stands to gain as well as lose, where the trade-offs may be, what are your absolute red lines, what is the line-up of forces amongst the other member states and where the Commission is coming from. If you are not going to run the risk of being totally blindsided or outflanked you have in the end to be prepared to put in the hours. Of course if you are a hardened Eurosceptic just waiting for the 'in-out' referendum which will allow us to regain our sovereignty you may not want to confer legitimacy on the EU by being seen to darken its doors. But that's a pretty high-risk strategy if in the meantime the EU – for better or worse – has the ability to fundamentally affect your department's work.

Finally, there is one other key Euro dimension which you have to be on top of, which is whether you and your department are punching your weight in the Whitehall Euro stakes. It is tempting to think that the only EU successes or disasters that may befall you will all be made in Brussels or Strasbourg. Not a bit of it. There is a big Euro machine here at home, based in the Cabinet Office, which exists to coordinate UK policy towards the EU. It advises the Prime Minister and the Foreign Secretary on the trade-offs, the negotiations, the concessions, the bottom lines and much more. It has to; there are just too many occasions when not every UK aim can be pursued, not every unhelpful development can be blocked and some cherished objectives have to be sacrificed in order to secure others.

Now if you are in the Treasury or the Foreign Office you can be pretty sure that your department is going to be a heavyweight in such discussions. But you can't assume that in Education; in Culture, Media and Sport; and in many others. Of course the really important decisions will come to ministers. But by the time they do the die will often be pretty well cast. So you need personally to know where No. 10, the Foreign Office and the Treasury are coming from and you need personally to be prepared to engage in the critical Whitehall battles. It also really matters whether your department has a handful of key officials who really 'get' the EU; who preferably speak some of the key EU languages between them; who know their counterparts in the other key member states and the European Commission; who are known and listened to in UKREP – the UK's 'embassy' to the EU based in Brussels whose members do much of the detailed negotiation on individual dossiers – and who, most importantly of all, carry real weight in the key departments in Whitehall. Otherwise you risk continually being the 'concession' being offered up for somebody else's benefit. So it is also well worth putting a conversation about the strength of your own department's EU team on the agenda for one of your regular catch-up sessions with the Permanent Secretary; even better to meet the key officials yourself to help form your own judgement.

So there it is. *C'est tout* ('that's all'). *Pièce de gateau.* You are now equipped to play a role in the EU business of your department which will marry the wisdom of Churchill with the resolution of De Gaulle. Or was it the other way round? *Bon chance*!

CHAPTER 17

# MAJOR PROJECTS

*There are two ways to write error-free programs. Only the third one works.*

LAWS OF COMPUTER PROGRAMMING I

As if you haven't got enough on your plate dealing with the party, the politics, Parliament and people of every description, it is suddenly dawning on you that your department is running some very big, and very scary, projects. They may not be on quite the scale of the Olympics or Universal Credit but they certainly have the capacity to go badly wrong and take your reputation down with them.

It may, of course, be that you're that rare breed of minister who actually has experience – real experience (the three-week attachment you once had under the Westminster and industry scheme doesn't unfortunately count) – of major project management in your life before politics. If so, please skip to the next chapter. But if (as much more likely) not, then read on.

First, a little bit of reassurance. One of the more enduring myths of twenty-first century Britain is that almost all major public sector projects fail and that the hapless civil servants running them have the combined experience of Noddy and Mr Bean. The truth is less entertaining but more reassuring. There are in fact many examples of successfully delivered public sector projects – of which the Olympics was but one – delivered by some highly experienced and competent people. Indeed most serious research shows no material difference between project success rates in the private and public sectors.

But even if that helps don't be overly reassured. Delivering big projects well – particularly if they are heavily dependent on IT – is seriously hard and the ones you have just come across in your new department are all likely to be high risk. If they are also costly and high profile the risks to you and your department simply multiply. You can no doubt remember all the 'shambles' and 'fiasco' headlines about some of the more recent examples. Indeed some of the lurid language you happily put in your own press notices while in opposition about the ones in the department you were shadowing may yet come back to haunt you.

So what can you do? Not, certainly, to try to micromanage any of the key projects yourself. Even if you had the time or inclination it would almost certainly end in tears. But that doesn't mean that you can't make a difference or exert some real influence. So here, as a starter, are four 'dos' and four 'don'ts'.

'Do' number 1. Show some real interest. There is a fine line between total indifference – until of course the day it all goes pear-shaped – and micro-management but the former is as likely to end up badly as the latter. At the very least you need to understand at a high level what the project is trying to do; what are the key things that it has to deliver and by when, and what are the key risks. So set aside some serious time in your diary – at least an hour for a first session – and get the key people in your office. Make sure that they include the Project director and the so-called 'Senior Responsible Owner', of whom more anon. Don't start off with a third-degree interrogation; it will merely encourage them into the bunker – but instead ask them to describe to you, honestly, the project's progress and risks. The more open they are the more you should thank them, even if what you're being told is uncomfortable. You have to establish an atmosphere of trust if you really want to find out what's going on. Above all, ask what more you and your ministers can do to increase the chances of the project's success. You may be surprised at what they tell you. And don't make this a one-off conversation; particularly for really big projects arrange to have regular catch-up sessions every three months or so.

'Do' number 2. Insist on being consulted personally by your Permanent Secretary before either the Project director or 'Senior Responsible Owner' is changed. These are the two most crucial people on any project. The role of the first is self-evident; he or she is the person who has to deliver the project successfully. The second – and you probably know this already – is the person in your department, normally very senior, who is personally responsible for ensuring that all of the resources and skills are in place to enable the project to succeed. Their role is absolutely key. They are in effect the bridge between the project and the rest of the department. They are there to tell the hard truths; to you and the Permanent Secretary if the project is in danger of failing for lack of resource or support; to the Project director if they and their team are simply not doing well enough; to the Cabinet Office, Treasury and the Major Projects Authority if their interventions are making success less rather than more likely.

Now there can be good reasons as to why one or other of these people should change during the lifetime of a project, particularly, for example, if the Project director proves not up to the task. But some very good work by the NAO – it's worth getting your private office to dig it out for you – shows that one of the most frequent contributors to projects failing is key people being changed along the way. Your very strong starting point should be that, unless there is a very good reason, you want to keep the same key people in place right through to the (hopefully not bitter) end. Indeed simply making clear that that is your view will make it much less likely that unjustifiable changes will take place.

'Do' number 3. Ask to receive a regular one-side (insist that you really mean one side) report direct from either the Project director or Senior Responsible Owner on progress including what has gone well or badly. And when you get it, read it.

How regular is regular? Weekly is almost certainly too frequent. Longer than monthly is almost certainly too infrequent. The key point is to have some quick means of keeping a personal eye on progress. Even more important emphasise to whoever is going to write the report for you that it's got to be candid and honest. Make clear that you won't ever lose your rag on account of people telling you the truth but you may well do so if they don't. And then keep to that. Don't feel incidentally that you have to get terribly excited, and start summoning people in, every time you read anything less than perfect. All projects have their ups and downs. Use your judgement. But if you are seriously worried about something you read then ask the key people to come and talk you through it.

'Do' number 4 is to keep asking about the 'c' word; in this case 'contingency'. An old but still extremely useful maxim in the world of project management is to hope for the best but plan for the worst. The only thing you can be certain of in big projects is that some elements will go wrong or not work as planned. That needn't be a disaster but is much more likely to be if there is no contingency plan for when it happens. So keep asking the Project director and the Senior Responsible Owner about the existence and adequacy of their contingency plans. You will probably want to politely decline if they offer to send them to you – though it's a good sign in that it suggests that they at least exist – given that they are likely to be too long and too detailed for you to get your head round. But what you can do – see 'don't' number 2 below – is to ask for the adequacy of the contingency plans to be reviewed as part of any external assessment that is carried out on the project as a whole.

Now for the 'don'ts'.

Number 1 is to set unrealistic and arbitrary deadlines. The litany of failed public sector projects which have passed into legend – like the original creation of the Child Support Agency and the Criminal Records Bureau – is replete with examples of where ministers demanded, often for good political reasons, that projects deliver ahead of what those responsible for delivering them thought possible. As in so much else there is a balance here; officials can be over-cautious and you are entitled to ask whether it really is going to take up until 2050 to deliver the new third runway at Heathrow. But be very wary indeed of simply issuing an instruction that something must be done by a given date irrespective of what you are being told about whether it can in fact be done. There is a fine line in this respect between strength and stupidity.

Even more difficult is if, having set a deadline for implementation, you are told that it needs to be put back. If it is a high-profile project that will almost certainly lead to political embarrassment and it may well cause a cost overrun as well. You are certainly entitled to probe the reasons for any proposed delay very hard and to ask for a second opinion (see 'Don't' number 2 below) but in the end the only thing worse than having to stand up in the House and explain why delivery is having to be delayed is having to stand up in the House to explain why, although the project was apparently delivered on time, it has rapidly become a total shambles.

'Don't' number 2 is linked in many ways to 'don't' number 1. Don't ever be afraid to get a second opinion. All well-run projects will have built in to their delivery timetable a series of periodic external assessments of progress. They can be really valuable and you should ask to see them whenever they take place. But if you are seriously concerned about progress more generally, or if you are being asked to make a key decision such as whether to agree to a delay and you lack confidence in whether you are really in a position to come to a sound conclusion, you are fully entitled to ask for an external assessment from an independent and respected source. Who that should best be will vary according to the nature of the question and the issue, and you will almost certainly want to discuss it with your Permanent Secretary and with whoever leads on major project monitoring in either the Cabinet Office or the Treasury. But it will almost never be a wasted effort; far better that you get a really good external view, even if an unwelcome one, while there is still time to act on the results than when you are reading the inevitable external assessment months or even years later as to why the project ended in disaster.

'Don't' number 3 is not to demand constant changes to the scope and detail of the project once these have been set. Another of the NAO's very powerful learning points about why projects fail is because those delivering them are forever having to make changes during the course of the project. If you liken the project to a 747 over the Atlantic you can begin to get the picture. You would no more ask someone to make improvements to the engines during flight than you would go up to the cockpit and ask to land the plane yourself. But that is pretty much the equivalent of changing the project specification once the project is already underway. There will always be good reasons why someone is asking for something to be added or changed. In themselves they may be highly desirable or politically advantageous. In the case of major projects they may come from key stakeholders like No. 10. But you need both to restrain yourself and restrain others. If you don't the likelihood of the 747 disaster will be much the greater.

The final 'don't' – number 4 – is not to sign off quickly on major new projects which are going to require brand-new cutting-edge IT systems no matter how much you are assured that they are well within our capacity to deliver and will bring with them benefits to rival the splendours of the ancient world. They are also much more likely than not to fail – keep asking about the NHS IT programme – or, even if they eventually succeed, to do so only years late and over budget. You may hear much said in this context, somewhat dismissively, about your having to rely otherwise on your so-called 'legacy' systems which are always implied, though never actually said, to be on the point of finally falling over never to be stood back up again. But remember one thing about your department's 'legacy' systems; they actually work. Adapting and building on them can be much less glamorous, and more limiting, but as the private sector have found is also much more likely to succeed. If you keep asking about the alternatives to cutting-edge new technology you are, in the end, likely to be offered some.

So there you have it. Some 'dos'. Some 'don'ts'. But even doing, or not doing, them all is no guarantee of success. If the gods are against you, you may still find yourself going to the House to explain the failure. But you will, by following them, at least reduce the risk of having to make that journey. And that's probably about the best you can hope for.

CHAPTER 18

# AGENCIES AND NDPBs

*As minister I accept the responsibility but not the blame.*

ROBERT SEMPLE (1873–1955), ON THE OCCASION OF AN INQUIRY IN 1944 INTO THE FORDELL TUNNEL 'BOTCH'

THE RE-ROUTING OF THE RAILWAY line between Turakina and Fordell on the North Island of New Zealand finally opened in 1947 having involved the construction, over a period of ten years, of three tunnels totalling 3.5 kilometres. A 2010 paper from the BECA engineering consultancy on the Repair and Modification of New Zealand Railway Tunnels between 1867 and 1980 noted that during construction of the Fordell tunnel its lining 'exhibited substantial cracking and distress leading to strengthening via the construction of a haunch in the lower walls'. It may, or may not, have been this that caused, or contributed to, the substantial delays in construction which occurred. What is clearly true, however, is that the New Zealand Minister of Works during World War Two, Robert Semple, was not prepared to take the rap even if he accepted the responsibility. Bizarrely, during his time in office he also designed and built a tank out of corrugated iron – known as the 'Bob Semple' – presumably to act as a further line of defence if someone still tried to pin the blame on him.

That tension between responsibility for setting the goal and delivering the outcome runs, like the Fordell tunnel fault line, through all modern government. The creation of Agencies and NDPBs has been one attempt – at some times more successful than others – to separate out responsibility for deciding what should happen, which remains with ministers, from responsibility for actually delivering it which, at least in theory, can be laid off to an arm's-length body, either an Agency or NDPB, rather than being directly delivered from within the core department. If you didn't know it already you are likely to have found out pretty quickly that you have at least one Agency and/or one or more NDPBs within the overall responsibility of your department. Indeed some departments – like Culture, Media and Sport – have literally dozens.

Now it would be wonderful to believe, like Robert Semple, that you are thus absolved from all blame, if not responsibility, if anything which any of your department's agencies or NDPBs does goes pear-shaped. The only problem is that it isn't remotely true. On the day when the proverbial hits the fan it's still likely to be your face on the front pages as your political opponents scream for your head. So best to give a bit of thought now to how to try to ensure that the worst doesn't happen or, if it does, that you at least have as good a story as possible to tell.

First of all, a crash course in the differences between an Agency and an NDPB (or to give it its full title a 'non-departmental public body'; only in Britain could we define such a key group of organisations by what they are not). The answer is that you could – and people already do – write reams on just that. So, for example, the staffs of Agencies are normally civil servants; the staffs of NDPBs normally aren't. The Chief Executive of an Agency normally reports directly to the Permanent Secretary or one of their deputies; the Chief Executive of an NDPB normally reports to a chair and a board, though just to add confusion the Chief Executive of an Agency may report to a chair and board as well. Though both are meant to be at arm's length from you and the department, the arm is generally longer in the case of an NDPB.

But the truth is that, other than to constitutional anoraks, the differences are often more apparent than real. Whether it be an Agency or an NDPB, if one of your arm's-length bodies suddenly finds itself, like the Environment Agency during the flooding in early 2014, at the centre of public controversy, you are going to find yourself inevitably drawn into that controversy, and probably being asked to shoulder blame as well as responsibility. So what should you do to ensure that if and when that happens you are not completely taken by surprise? Five things above all.

First, find out which Agencies and NDPBs your department is responsible for. That may sound breathtakingly obvious. But you would probably be surprised to learn that there have been ministers who had barely heard of some of their department's Agencies or NDPBs until the day when they found themselves reading about them on the front pages. So get your private office to give you the full list and some very brief details on each. And if it's a very long list, discuss with the Permanent Secretary and your special advisers which ones you need to focus on personally. For the rest make sure that one of your junior ministers is explicitly assigned responsibility for each one no matter how insignificant they may seem. The Weights and Measures Inspection Agency – for all we know there may actually be one – sounds bewilderingly dull until the day you find out that they've accepted, without reference to you, an EU proposal to rename the pint the 'Eurodrink'.

Second, for the bodies on the list which you decide to focus on personally, make a point of meeting the Chief Executive, and in the case of an NDPB the chair also, at regular intervals. You will be surprised at how often you learn things when you meet people face to face that you won't find out about from reading any number of deeply tedious submissions at the bottom of your box late at night. And when you do meet them, apart from trying hard to look interested – even weights and measures can have their fascination – always ask the naive question 'so what are you worrying about at the moment?' As long as you can manage to do so in a way that doesn't convey a threat of menace if they tell you what they really are worrying about you may be surprised at how open they'll be. And even if it's all rather worrying, far better that you hear about it before it's all over the front pages and while there is an opportunity to do something about it.

Third, if you can possibly find the time go out and see it, whatever it is. How easy or difficult that is will, of course, depend on what it does and where it does it but there's almost always something worth seeing and some people worth meeting. Not only will that stand you in good stead on the day when you do find yourself having to deal with the problem, but it will often accrue you a remarkably large amount of good-will in return for quite a small investment of your time. The strange thing is people will really want to see and meet you, and you may just enjoy it. You will also learn far more by actually going to see it. Better than the boxes surely.

Fourth, pay heed to any obvious warning signs. If you start seeing a regular flow of complaints about what the body is doing in your ministerial postbag ask for a report on what the problems are and how they are being addressed. If your department's Select Committee is becoming sufficiently concerned to hold a hearing on the body's performance don't treat that as simply being run of the mill. If something is beginning to smell wrong – even if you're getting lots of reassuring noises from the Chief Executive and their board – consider with the Permanent Secretary whether you may want to commission some form of external review. It may confirm that there is indeed no major cause for concern. But that in itself will be valuable.

Fifth, and finally, satisfy yourself that the performance of each such body in your department is being regularly monitored and that there is a clear responsibility for stewardship and oversight at senior level. Nothing is more likely to end in tears than a body whose actions and activities have simply fallen off the radar with the result that no one external to the body itself has any clue what it is or is not achieving. Of course, this can beg the question of what you should do if the body is clearly under-performing, or if you simply find yourself never acquiring or losing confidence in the Chief Executive or chair, or both, of the body concerned. Now that will clearly depend on degree. It would be surprising if you never have any cause for qualms or concerns over some aspect or other of what they are doing. In general micro-management in such circumstances is a pretty bad idea, even if you have the skills or knowledge to substitute your judgement for those running the organisation. But equally if you do have a fundamental lack or loss of confidence in the current leadership it is probably wise to talk to the Permanent Secretary about the possibilities of effecting a change. That may well not be easy but, in the end, backing your own judgement will probably be the right call.

Of course, none of this answers the more fundamental question as to whether it makes sense for a particular Agency or NDPB to continue at all and, if so, in its current form. There are, or at least were, supposed to be Cabinet Office processes for considering just that reasonably regularly. Indeed your own government may have committed itself to a bonfire of quangos or whatever other similar epithet you came up with in opposition. And it does make sense periodically to stand back and ask what this body is actually there for and what would happen if it simply didn't exist.

Equally, be prepared to ask yourself honestly whether you really are willing to delegate decisions, and real authority, to the body in question. If in the end, as Secretary of State for Education, you want the final say as to what will be taught in our schools, then it will almost certainly end in tears to purport to give the authority to make those decisions to an arm's-length quango. Far better in those circumstances to have the honesty to bring the function back in-house under your direct control.

But be wary equally of constant tinkering with structures, names and responsibilities. Announcing that you are bringing the Weights and Measures Inspection Agency back within your core department because you happen to dislike one or two particular decisions it has made, or alternatively renaming it as 'Weightsplus' – 'a twenty-first-century body for the twenty-first century', may get you a few column inches but is far more likely simply to divert the entire organisation's attention from what you actually want it to do. There will be enough people wanting to redesign the corporate logo without you adding to it. Concentrating on the substance rather than the superficial is almost always the better choice.

And if all else fails you can always build a tank. The designs for the 'Bob Semple' are still to be found on the internet.

CHAPTER 19

# NO. 10

*I met Curzon in Downing Street from whom I got the sort of greeting a corpse would give to an undertaker.*

STANLEY BALDWIN (1867–1947) ON BECOMING PRIME MINISTER

THERE ARE LOTS OF BOOKS written about how No. 10 works; or doesn't and should be improved. This chapter isn't one of them. Instead, it's about how you deal with No. 10 from the outside, how you relate to the Prime Minister who appointed you.

Of course, that depends on the kind of No. 10 that you're dealing with. There are many myths about No. 10. That it is too strong. That it is too political. In fact, from the inside, the most striking thing about No. 10 is how weak its powers are. Essentially, the PM's only power is to appoint. And he has fewer people working for him than the typical director in DWP. The Treasury, for example, is represented on every Cabinet Committee and sub-committee but not the Prime Minister.

So, you need to start by taking the measure of No. 10. Sometimes, No. 10 will be so weak that they won't be able to help or stop you doing anything much – but that is normally at the end of a government, so you may not be able to push through any major reforms anyway. In those circumstances, find some middling things to do, try to build consensus with other parties, as Andrew Adonis did with High Speed Rail in the dog days of the last Labour government.

But this is the exception. Most of the time you'll be dealing with a No. 10 that can decide whether your precious initiative sees the light – and whether your next job is a promotion or a consolation.

We know what makes up an effective No. 10. A small but high-powered core team, so that Whitehall knows that when they say 'the Prime Minister wants...' they've actually spoken to the Prime Minister this year. They need a few levers to pull – a Delivery Unit by whatever name to improve performance, a Strategy Unit to crack cross-cutting problems. In theory, it would be good to move into a new building, but it's no more likely than the Queen moving out of Buckingham Palace.

Despite the bluster, we also know how Whitehall should work. Cabinet Committees have more of a role than the Blair government initially gave them. But that role is not all-encompassing. They are good at trying to create consensus where that is what is needed. But, as we remark in our chapter on Cabinet colleagues, they risk finding lowest common denominator solutions.

So Cabinet Committees need to be supplemented by other policy meetings. They can be formal – such as the regular stocktakes which Tony Blair used to take for the departments that were carrying out his key priorities. Or they can be informal – there's nothing wrong with a Secretary of State and a Prime Minister simply chatting about what they're up to. The key is to recognise that the latter is better for creating shared assumptions than for taking formal decisions about the future of Trident or whether to enter the Euro.

So, let's posit a No. 10 that works in this way. How should you deal with them? With proportion. The greatest danger is to get the perspective wrong, and either think that No. 10 are thinking about you all the time, or not at all.

The hard truth is that most of the time No. 10 will have only the vaguest idea what you're doing. When the Prime Minister appoints you as Secretary of State, he'll certainly know who you are and what job he's appointing you to, but not necessarily what he wants you to do. When he calls to appoint you, let him do the talking – if he wants you to do something, he'll say so. If not, just remember he's making another twenty similar calls that morning, and needs to get them all done before the lunchtime news. Tony Blair, for example, would write to every newly appointed Cabinet minister with his list of top priorities for their departments. Most found that helpful, particularly where they were on the same wavelength. Others might have found them much more challenging. But either way, it is better to know what is on the Prime Minister's mind at the outset rather than only to discover that you are heading in completely different directions later on. In these cases, only one of you is likely to have to change course.

But that doesn't mean you should just hide in obscurity. If no one at No. 10 knows what or how you're doing, then your ministerial career may be rather short. As we note in our very last chapter some people have to make way each reshuffle so that new talent can be promoted, or troublemakers bought off, and you don't want to be the makeweight.

So, try to identify a couple of key allies at No. 10. The expert on your department in the Policy Unit is a good place to start. They'll probably be the one writing a note at reshuffle time to say how each minister in the department is doing – to complement the thoughts of the Cabinet Secretary, based on their Permanent Secretaries' views (that's a thought worth keeping lodged in your head...)

Build a relationship with your Policy Unit person. You can help each other. They need you to make sure the department does what the Prime Minister wants. You need them to write approving submissions to the Prime Minister about your policy ideas and White Papers. They may even have some good ideas that you could work on together. A regular catch-up is good – invite them to team meetings. Within reason let them see any papers they want.

Many ministers, and Permanent Secretaries, worry about what the Policy Unit will find out if left to roam around the department unsupervised. In fact, it's really the Prime Minister who should worry more about capture of their special advisers. Give them all the access they want, and they're just as likely to become your advocate inside No. 10. Of course, the best special advisers manage to be both – on your side when you're right, but the Prime Minister's when he is – or thinks he is.

This is particularly true at Spending Review time. The Whitehall scrabble for resources will be reproduced in the Policy

Unit. Human nature shouldn't be like this, but no one is going to want to be the adviser who doesn't get anything for their departments. So, if it's a small policy unit, and each adviser has two or three departments, make sure you're at the top of their pile. Involve them in the writing of the spending review papers. Put their pet ideas in, maybe at a bit above cost to create some headroom for your own. And then work together. It's rare not to be able to find £50 million extra down the back of the Downing Street sofa.

And remember that, unlike their junior ministers, Secretaries of State have not only to decide the strategy for their department, but also to share the burden for the political strategy of the government. Whitehall is often compared to an ocean liner and, if that is accurate, then becoming a Secretary of State is a bit like going from arranging the deck furniture to being responsible for where the ship is going, how it's maintained and refuelled, staffed and what to do about those Somali pirates.

So, you need to realise that your responsibilities have changed. The key responsibility for the relationship with No. 10 is yours. If you don't tell the PM and his team what your department is doing, no one else will – except the newspapers and the opposition when it all goes wrong. And if you don't tell your junior ministers what the political strategy of the government is, ditto. When the government hits a crisis, it's your job to make sure that everyone knows the line, and is signed up to it. In return, you need to protect your ministers – politics can be a scary place, and even the thickest skinned will value a Secretary of State who stands up for them when the inevitable squalls come along.

And don't forget what you read in the documents the Permanent Secretary gave you when you were promoted. Which documents? Your private office can get you another copy. There was something in there about the doctrine of collective responsibility – the Cabinet agree with the whole of the government's policy. That's why you get the right to be consulted about it – but the other side of that coin is that you should do what you can to defend that policy within government. It's easy to go back to your department and just raise your eyebrows at the latest wheeze. But that's the way that governments start to die.

And don't be shy about dealing with the PM direct. His only formal power is that of patronage, remember. He needs his Cabinet to support him, or at least most of it to support him, most of the time. And he also needs a core that supports him all of the time. Work out how the PM likes to communicate – Tony Blair thought through circular conversations, often on the phone on Sundays or from the car. Try to get yourself in on some of those, become a sounding board, be candid about problems, but also someone who solves them rather than exacerbates them. If that goes well, push for a regular stocktake, where you report on performance and agree next steps. Make sure any public event that you do together is perfectly planned and shorter than the diary allowed.

But that's the ideal ... it doesn't always work like that. Many are the ministers who thought they were doing fine, only to find that reshuffle call is of the sympathetic kind. If you're not getting any feedback from No. 10 once you're in the Cabinet, then you do need to work out whether it's because the PM just isn't interested in agriculture, or because he thinks you're doing an awful job but can't bring himself to tell you face to face.

That's if the Prime Minister is prepared to see you face to face. He may think you are trying to get his job. His adviser may be telling him to sack you. He may well want to. But if he does, you need to do two things. First, defend yourself. When one Cabinet minister started to read briefings against himself he walked into the Chief Whip's office and said that if there was a single further article, he would be breaking his silence and doing a blizzard of interviews. The briefing stopped. But however bad the relationship, there's still a government to run. You need to do business together. So the second thing you need to work out is who is the best conduit if you haven't got your own channel – it might well be your Permanent Secretary talking to the Cabinet Secretary, particularly if they both get on. It might be your special advisers talking to each other. Tommy McAvoy, Labour's legendary pairing Whip, used to say that 'we all have our different relationships' – just because two advisers work for ministers who are sworn enemies, doesn't mean they don't get on. They may have been in student politics together, they might play for the party's football team. Find the way to keep communications open – it may not be the Vatican keeping channels open in the Middle East, but it's still important.

One final thought: try to avoid saying anything that gets quoted by the leader of the opposition back to the Prime Minister at PMQs. That tends to be bad.

Now, back to those priorities.

## CHAPTER 20

# CABINET COLLEAGUES

*All government, indeed every human benefit and enjoyment, every virtue and every prudent act, is founded on compromise and barter.*

EDMUND BURKE (1729–1797)

IT'S TIME TO STEP OUTSIDE the department. It's hard. You've got comfortable here. People tend to agree with you. If they don't, you can always over-rule them.

Going to a meeting with another Cabinet colleague can be quite a shock. You've both spent a good few weeks working out your policy, and then you find that the Department of Health is arguing for A, against your B. Your private offices suggest a meeting between you. But one of you is going to have to climb down. Do that too often, and going back to the department won't feel quite as comfortable – a minister who can't get their way outside will start finding things getting harder inside.

As the old joke goes, if you've ended up here, you've started from the wrong place. You've allowed your relationship with your Cabinet colleagues to become secondary to your relationship with your department. Of course, your civil servants matter. But you're a politician. You were elected as part of a team of politicians, and your primary duty is to represent your voters and implement the programme which you stood on.

It was different in opposition. You spent most of your time together. You saw other shadow ministers all day, in Parliament, campaigning, in strategy meetings. But then you won – and now you find yourself cocooned in your ministerial office and your ministerial car. The camaraderie of opposition cools. Some of the original shadow Cabinet leave – the first resignations. Younger MPs get promoted. In opposition, you spent two thirds of your waking day with other MPs – in meetings, the Tea Room, the Chamber. Today, two thirds of your day is taken up with stakeholders and departmental meetings.

'Exactly!' we hear you protest. 'I'd like to spend more time talking to other ministers. But when!? 3 a.m., before I start on my box?'

Deep breath. Let's leave to one side whether you like your colleagues. We probably shouldn't go there. Or whether you are interested in their ideas. This is probably unlikely. Let's just concentrate on time. From a pure time-management perspective, you should spend less time in your department, and more time with other Cabinet colleagues.

'Relationships precede action'. One of the first rules of community organisation: a group that gets on together can do anything; a group that hates itself can't do anything. Take the decision about whether to bid for the Olympics. Tessa Jowell was strongly in favour – but she needed to convince the rest of the Cabinet. She went round each of her colleagues – John Reid told her at full volume that he feared it was a mad idea; but that he would support her, because it was her. That's not suspending judgement – it's trusting people you respect, and recognising that we achieve more together than we do alone. One of us, John, did the same thing when the government was trying to decide the right way forward on pension reform in 2006 in speaking to all of his Cabinet colleagues in one-to-one meetings to explain what he was trying to do. The distinct impression from fellow ministers was that this did not happen very often, which just confirmed how isolated ministers had become from each other.

So, from a pure time-management point of view, see your colleagues as often as you can. But don't ask your private office to sort the meetings out. When you're arranging to see a friend, or your husband, do you get your secretary to call them? No – you do it yourself. It's the same with colleagues – they may or may not be your close friends; but you definitely want to have a human relationship, not a bureaucratic one. It makes working together that much more straightforward. And in any case, if your private office fixes the meeting, they will come, take a minute, keep an eye on the time, because the 'informal' meeting will have been squeezed in for thirty minutes before PMQs, and it will feel anything other than informal.

Go for dinner. Not in the Commons. Even better – go and do something fun. You both like theatre – see a play together. Football? Go to a match. Anything, other than sitting awkwardly in a ministerial office being stared at by officials who will all be wondering what on earth is going on.

Of course, if you're doing that just to use your time efficiently, it won't work. Ideally, you like each other, share some values and are jointly committed to the success of your party. That may sound naive. But even if the relationship isn't ideal, try to act decently – and if you can't manage that, see if at least your special advisers can get on. Even if the politicians leading two departments are at each other's throats, there is business to be done. Being a grown-up means finding a way of facilitating the business of government even if you disagree on most things.

That's not to say that camaraderie should replace Cabinet government. It is to say that it's necessary to make Cabinet government work. Without it, Cabinet sub-committees become ossified, with everyone turning up simply to read out their pre-established positions, and with the secretariat left to cobble together a position from the bits to which no one objected. That kind of lowest common denominator politics is death – we could have done A, or we could have done B – both had some merit – but instead we chose a mongrel of the unobjectionable bits of each. Establishing effective relationships means you have a decent prospect of having a political conversation that gets to a good answer.

But is that enough? Can Cabinet government work when Cabinet ministers all work in separate buildings? Australia and New Zealand point to a different structure. There ministers spend much of their time in the same building – in Parliament in Canberra, and in the splendidly named 'beehive' – go there, it really looks like one – in Wellington. This latter example is particularly interesting – the Cabinet are all located in a building that has been added to the side of the Parliament. So, the ministers see each other all the time. New Zealand ministers say that that alone has prevented more crises than all the official processes. There are potential downsides of course – an us-and-them mentality could develop between the minister and their department – though that can happen anyway. And the risk would be that it would be harder to develop those really good relationships with key officials which sometimes come about simply by virtue of working so closely with them. But the powerful upside would be that ministers wouldn't lose that 'band of brothers' feeling when they go into government. In Part II of our book on lessons learned we argue that this is a model we should at least seriously consider.

By now you're probably thinking about the one Cabinet colleague with whom you can't stand being stuck in a lift, let alone sharing an office or a beehive. But is that the symptom or the cause? Most of those problems stem from small policy differences, hardened into correspondence, corroded into a row, publicised by a leak, to be avenged at some unspecified time. This is a surprisingly easy place to end up. Perhaps if you'd just bumped into each other in a lift, that chain would have been broken. Anyway – it's just a thought.

But whatever you think about the structural solution, don't forget the rest. After all, the political is the personal. Don't be too quick to sign the withering letter to your Cabinet colleague; don't assume that your department must be right and theirs must be wrong; don't allow yourself to fall all too easily into that siege mentality; it might just be that you can achieve more together than apart. That really is the simple message of this short chapter.

CHAPTER 21

# 'GOATS' (OR A 'GOVERNMENT OF ALL THE TALENTS')

*Everybody has talent at twenty-five. The difficult thing is to have it at fifty.*

EDGAR DEGAS (1834–1917)

THEN, JUST WHEN YOU THINK it can't get any worse, the Prime Minister's Principal Private Secretary rings to say that the PM is 'thinking about' inviting someone he really admires from outside politics to join the government and is wondering whether there might not be a post for them in your department. Ignore the euphemisms; the correct translation is that the PM has been talking to the person concerned for weeks, if not months, and has already offered them the job but has suddenly realised, or more likely been reminded by the Cabinet Secretary, that he needs to square it with you before making the announcement.

This doesn't have to be bad news – there are cases of outsiders succeeding in government, particularly where the outsider is a respected specialist in their field but without pretensions of grandeur – but on past evidence it is at least as likely to end in tears as not. So a key question is whether No. 10 and the PM are absolutely fixed on the idea. If not, you may be able to plant the seed that while this would, of course, be an inspired appointment, it might be even better if the person in question was to be appointed to a department other than yours. But let's pause for a moment and consider first the track record of bringing outsiders into government.

It is, of course, not a wholly new idea. Over the years it's been particularly popular with the Royals – Henry II appointing Thomas Becket as Archbishop of Canterbury; Richard III relying on the Duke of Northumberland to support him at the Battle of Bosworth; and Henry VIII chumming up with Thomas More – though they aren't hugely encouraging precedents as Thomas More might have confirmed as he was led to the scaffold. More recently Churchill was all for enlisting the support of outsiders – like De Gaulle, General Sikorski and even Stalin – though again they didn't all turn out to be quite as supportive of UK interests as he might have hoped. On the other hand, there are more serious examples from history of where outsiders have been notably successful: Sir Joseph Maclay, the Glasgow-born shipping magnate, at the Ministry of Shipping in the Great War, Beaverbrook being put in charge of aircraft production in World War Two and Sir John Anderson, whose place in history stems largely from having given his name to the 'Anderson' shelter, as Lord President and then Chancellor in that same conflict. More recently, David (later Lord) Young who Margaret Thatcher brought into her Cabinet from business in the early 1980s – 'other ministers bring me problems, David brings me solutions' – undoubtedly brought ideas, energy and determination. What tends to mark out the instances where outsiders succeed is where they have skills or experience which politicians and civil servants simply do not have, where there is a genuine need for those skills and where they have the ability in turn to harness and appreciate the skills of the insiders they find themselves working with.

But the failures are at least as numerous. This may be because there is something of an innate problem here. Most of those brought into government as Goats in recent years have spent their lives getting to the top – be they captains of industry, highly decorated generals or self-made millionaires. They tend, by definition, to have acquired pretty large egos – if there were a recognised international ego measurement scale most would be in danger of falling off the end – and they are used to having those egos serially flattered. What they are most certainly not used to doing is following other people's orders or, much worse, toeing the party line. They are accustomed to calling a spade a spade, not indulging in long-winded euphemisms, still less ducking the question.

Now all of these are fine and valued qualities; were it not for the fact that they are not always so in the rather ambiguous world of government. Most ministers – whatever else may distinguish them – have learned the rules. Coalition politics aside, they do not go out of their way to disagree with government policy – still less the No. 10 line – on the *Today* programme; they tend not to jump in to the business of departments other than their own, certainly not publicly. And whatever they may think of their civil servants most do not think it a great idea to set out their failings on the record to any passing journalist. Goats, by contrast, tend to think that these rules are not for them. Indeed, didn't the Prime Minister, when they agreed to take on the job, tell them that he wanted them to speak their mind? So it comes as a rather hard landing to find that on the day they do go 'off message' they are rapidly forced by the same No. 10 that appointed them into an embarrassingly public U-turn.

Now, to be fair, there are present-day exceptions as well as exceptions from history. They tend, unsurprisingly, to be the more perceptive and thoughtful of their peers. They recognise that government is different and that they may need to adopt a different style in order to achieve their aims. They are more cautious in talking to journalists or in taking to the air waves. And they recognise that civil servants can actually help them navigate through the murky and sometimes turbulent waters of Whitehall. Most importantly of all they do not spend their time telling all and sundry how clever they are by contrast to almost everyone else around them.

However, we digress. How best to respond to the prospect of having a 'Goat' imposed upon you? One answer, of course, is to have got in first and appointed your own quasi Goat or Goats yourself. And there may be a much better case for doing so anyway. However good your ministerial team, and however expert (or not) your civil servants, it will be unusual if you conclude that you have all the expertise or intellectual muscle you need in-house. You may well want to think, in the one or two areas that really matter the most to you, of bringing in one or two genuine experts from outside to help you.

There are some risks in this, as we have set out in our separate chapter on analysis and experts. Both No. 10 and your Permanent Secretary are going to get pretty uncomfortable if they think you are simply trying to bring in another one or two special advisers by another name. You need also to ensure that anyone you bring in is going to want to work collaboratively with your ministerial team and your civil servants; don't believe all the guff about how good it is to have creative tension. Having real debate about ideas and policies is one thing, but having people at daggers drawn is simply a recipe for disaster. If you can avoid these pitfalls, however, having one or two genuinely expert advisers inside the department can be a real advantage. And it will make it easier on the day you do get the phone call from No. 10 about taking in a 'Goat' to simply hang out the 'No Vacancies' sign.

But if this isn't going to work, either because No. 10 are simply not to be moved or because you can't legitimately claim to have someone already covering the ground that the Goat is supposedly going to graze on, then you need to work out pretty quickly – and keep No. 10 at bay in the meantime – whether this is someone you can work with or not.

Returning to the earlier theme of the chapter, not a bad test is to regard the size of the prospective Goat's ego as being in inverse proportion to the chances of their appointment not ending in disaster; for which, incidentally, No. 10 will hold you personally responsible, quietly forgetting that it was all their idea in the first place. Put simply, the bigger the size of their ego, the harder they will be to control in any serious way and the more likely that someone at the end of it all will have to go.

So, if you don't know the individual well, sound out people who do or get your special advisers or the Permanent Secretary to do so on your behalf. And then meet them yourself – probably more than once if you don't already know them well – to get your own take on what kind of person they are and what is motivating them, apart from pure flattery, to come into government. Of course all this will be much harder to do, and the timescales much more compressed, if this is all happening in the context of a wider reshuffle. But even then try to retain some control over whether the appointment happens or not. Remind No. 10 of the old adage of appointing in haste and repenting at leisure. And remember that, unless your own job is on the line, in which case you have more important things to worry about, the Prime Minister will in the end be reluctant to impose someone on you over your dead body – particularly if you can suggest ways of making use of the individual's talent other than by making them a minister (asking them to produce a report for government on whatever it is they are meant to be expert in is a well-worn strategy but still one of the best).

But let's suppose that you are going to get a Goat either because you actually want them, or because the No. 10 pressure becomes irresistible. Even then there are still things you can and should do to increase the chances that their appointment will turn out to be a success rather than a disaster.

First, you need to actually find them something to do ('the devil makes work...' and all that). It should preferably be something real and genuinely in need of being done, but ideally not something which is going to put them immediately at odds with half of your Cabinet colleagues, nor require their daily appearance on the media. And you need to agree with them the specific things – 'deliverables' in the jargon – that they are going to produce and by when. With the Permanent Secretary's help, you also need to ensure that they are assigned an experienced and savvy civil servant as both their support and their 'minder'.

You also need to make very clear that you are in charge and lay down the ground rules. In particular make clear that you expect any media contacts to be cleared with you and either your media adviser or the department's chief press officer before they happen. That won't prevent such contacts happening without your knowledge, of course, but it is likely to reduce the number of times when it occurs. Even more important, make clear that you expect all contact with No. 10 to be similarly agreed with you in advance. And, in parallel, arrange to meet your Goat – probably weekly in their early days – so that you can keep in touch with what they are doing and offer them your support. They'll work out, of course, unless they are incredibly dense, that this is a control rather than a support mechanism, but no matter if it has the desired result. And ask your Permanent Secretary to similarly meet your Goat on a regular basis. One of the ironies is that however critical they may be of bureaucrats and bureaucracy in general they'll be a bit apprehensive about upsetting your very own Sir Humphrey.

Finally, seek to remind them, gently, that while they've been brought in to do an incredibly important job it does not actually give them the licence to comment publicly on every other aspect of government policy from nursery education to nuclear policy. And if and when they do, remind them of the conversation in a way which makes it at least unmistakable that you are not best pleased.

Now if all this sounds rather draconian, and a little cynical, that's because the risks are high. If in the end they don't materialise and it's clear that you've acquired someone not just of real experience and ability but also with some sophistication and political nous then you can call off the dogs and give them genuinely greater responsibility. But better to start tight and move to loose than to try moving the other way round.

And what do you do if, despite everything, it all does end in tears? Console yourself with the thought that you won't be the first or the last Secretary of State to have to explain that your Goat, who was indeed announced on their appointment as the greatest thing since sliced bread, has unfortunately gone walkabout and that, while you can understand the frustration that led to their public denunciation of the government, you fear that they have failed to see the bigger picture.

And next time, get your private office to tell No. 10 that it's someone else's turn to draw the short straw.

## CHAPTER 22

# OPPOSITION

*No government can be long secure without a formidable opposition.*

BENJAMIN DISRAELI (1804–1881)

SECRETARIES OF STATE HAVE TWO key responsibilities. They must be able to make decisions on policy. And they must then be able to explain, defend and justify this policy to a sceptical outside world. To do this second job well, you will need to be able to handle opposition. And – amazingly, given the obvious brilliance of your policy and the equally brilliant way in which you present it – opposition will come in all sorts of shapes and sizes and frequently from those who claim to be on your own side.

So perhaps the first thing to appreciate is that the

'opposition' does not always come with a capital 'O'. When you were in opposition, you will undoubtedly have spent a large part of your time trying to build up support for your ideas amongst some of the key organisations whose opinions were considered to be influential – trade unions, faith groups, charities, think tanks and so on. Many of them would have been happy to exchange views and to be taken seriously. Some might even have lent you their support, even though they might not have been in total agreement with every aspect of your policy, because as the opposition you would have provided a convenient and helpful crutch for them to lean on in their own arguments with the government. So much so that it can sometimes feel in opposition that everyone agrees with you that the government is doing the wrong thing. Surely then when it comes to your turn to occupy the great offices of State they will all be behind you?

Wrong. Opposition to most of the things you do as a minister will be the normal state of affairs and it will often come from those who before the election gave the impression of being your greatest friends. In a healthy democracy this is how it should be. No one gets a free ride. One of your biggest tests will be how you manage this inevitable and constant criticism. Unlike in opposition when your words might have sounded attractive to many organisations, it is now your deeds that you will be judged by and there is a world of difference between the two.

It is true that sometimes there is no way to minimise or negate genuine policy disagreements, and in some cases you will no doubt welcome the sound of opposition as it can provide helpful definition. In these cases you will need to argue your corner but you can at least try and avoid creating the impression that everyone who disagrees with you is either unpatriotic or stupid. The first rule is to respect your opponents and where there are genuine areas of disagreement to have sufficient confidence in your own decisions to avoid the path of insult and abuse. Try and remember, even in the heat of battle, how you look and sound to the public who are either watching you on TV, listening to you on the radio or, increasingly, learning about you from social media sites. Also try and keep in your mind that most of your opponents – simply by virtue of not being in government – probably enjoy more public confidence and credibility than you do and so are more likely to be believed than you are. In today's politics, being a Secretary of State counts for very little in the highly sceptical court of public opinion.

Coming into government there is now also a second de facto rule that needs to be strictly adhered to if you want to try and maximise support for your White Paper or legislation and deal with any possible opposition. It's called having to consult. Baroness Margaret Jay famously criticised many so-called consultation exercises as simply a period of time that elapses before ministers confirm their original intentions. It will help you enormously if you can avoid giving this impression. It will help even more if you actually mean it and are willing to change your mind in response to what people say. If you have been developing policy with a range of organisations in opposition, don't stop talking to them when you move into your new plush ministerial office. Ensure that your department does not become an impenetrable ivory tower. Keep the channels of communication open and ask your officials to engage with these organisations at the earliest stage of policy development. It won't guarantee that you will retain whatever good faith you were able to generate in opposition, but it will most certainly help. And remember always that there is a world of difference between these channels of communication and the more formal consultation that follows a White or Green Paper. These processes are important but have a more stage-managed and more formal dimension. Changing direction at these late stages in policy development is much harder to do.

How you maintain these open channels of communication is a matter for you to decide. You will almost certainly want to meet personally with the more important organisations that concern your department on a regular basis. If these relationships are genuinely important to you then your Diary Secretary must know that they need to stay in the diary even when the pressure inevitably starts to build up. Nothing loses goodwill faster than the last-minute never-ending changes to your diary which contrive to give the impression that your time matters and their time doesn't. And while your junior ministers, special advisers and officials can also help keep these outside organisations involved in the policy formulation process ahead of the publication of your formal proposals, there is in the end no substitute for giving them your own time.

Some of this can appear unbelievably tedious when all you want to do is get on with it. All former Secretaries of State will at times have become frustrated by what appears to them as wholly extended consultation being imposed on them by their officials as a means of delaying or diluting their own ideas – 'I fear, Minister, that there is a real prospect of judicial review unless we consult as a minimum with the British Treefellers' Association before we move ahead with your inspired plan to turn Epping Forest into a leisure park'. It can, however, provide a mechanism for garnering valuable support for the time when things get tough, as well as a process for ironing out the creases in your otherwise brilliant ideas.

On the other hand, it is perfectly possible (and almost certainly likely) that at times you are going to welcome an argument with your opponents over policy. You, after all, will want to change things and challenge the status quo created by your predecessor. In which case, there is a third rule to follow. Pick your arguments carefully and only have the ones you really must win if you are to progress your political priorities. Concentrate your political capital wisely and spend it only on the big-ticket items. These will be the issues that will define your mission as a minister or as a government and over which there can be no ambiguity or confusion. Only you can make these strategic judgements as they will be intricately linked to how you see the challenges ahead. And on some issues it is very hard to prepare the ground in advance of the argument – something it is generally sensible to do.

When Gordon Brown announced the government's decision to transfer interest rate policy to the Bank of England – a defining moment in every sense for the new Labour government – it was impossible to share the decision with anyone else for fear of creating a market impact. Nevertheless, the skilful way in which the argument was made both wrong-footed the opposition and won the admiration of independent commentators. But where it is possible to bring people along with you the opportunity should be taken. For example, the way the last Labour government set out its plans to modernise the NHS in 2000 was a model of its kind. All of the main patient care organisations signed up to the White Paper in advance in a unique endorsement of government policy, which had the effect of instantly marginalising the opposition and gaining a great deal of support in the media and elsewhere. Much more bruising, but equally effective, was the argument over unilateral nuclear disarmament led by Michael Heseltine when he was Defence Secretary in the early 1980s. It was an argument that was strategic in every sense, had a simple, easily understood message and was one that the Secretary of State obviously relished. Persuasive voices were organised in support of the government's case for retaining Britain's nuclear weapons posture and it was relentlessly rammed home, undermining the opposition's credibility in the eyes of most of the electorate.

On the other side of the equation there are plenty of examples of how not to conduct a big argument over strategy. The present government's reforms to the NHS are a case in point. Complicated reforms which few people understood, which were not shared in advance with anyone, which were so badly presented that they almost reached the point of collapse, and which were only saved from total parliamentary annihilation by enforced compromise and backtracking. Not a happy experience for anyone involved.

And then there's Parliament. Not all of the opposition you will face will be in Parliament, but a lot of it will be, and how you face up to it will be a key element in defining your success or failure. In Parliament – to which we have devoted an earlier chapter – handling the opposition is traditionally seen in gladiatorial terms. Alpha-male politicians locked in mortal combat. And there is a good deal of truth in this simple characterisation. But it doesn't tell the whole story and as a senior minister you will need at times to try and rise above the fray. There will be some issues affecting national security for example where you are absolutely required to talk to your shadow. There are other occasions where it can be incredibly useful.

One of us, John, recalls talking to his shadow DWP Secretary Philip Hammond in 2006 about Lord Turner's reforms to the pension system. Turner had proposed automatically enrolling employees into workplace pensions for the first time – a huge step to take when most of the existing arrangements had been voluntary. Philip Hammond straightaway indicated that he would support these proposals, clearing the way for the government to sustain a consensus over the future direction of policy in an area where, because of the long-term nature of any fundamental reforms to the pension system, this mattered a great deal. And what was more, he kept to his word. It was an eye-opening illustration of the value of talking to your opponents. The world did not come to an end. Quite the opposite. We all got into a much better place.

Of course the opposition in Parliament does not only come from the opposition benches. Opposition can easily build up on your own backbenches unless you are prepared to keep open a dialogue with your colleagues – many of whom privately think they could do a better job than you. Your Whip and PPS will have a role to play but it is often a thankless one because there is no substitute for talking directly to the Secretary of State. Only you can make this happen. One of the great political risks in becoming a minister is the sense of isolation that can easily develop between you and your backbench supporters. Never let yourself fall so deep into your departmental bunker that you lose sight of the world outside. Explain to your Permanent Secretary that while his proposal for you to hold a series of policy seminars with each of your key policy teams in turn over the next six months is truly inspired, you're not going to do it right at the moment. Come up for air every now and again. Keep in touch with backbench opinion. Even if you cannot reach agreement on everything it is at least better to be properly forewarned of trouble. And because you will be so immersed in the policy you are advocating it is very easy to dismiss these warnings if they reach you from other sources. It is much harder to be cavalier when you have heard the warnings at first hand.

Some of the opposition you face will come from even closer to home. Dealing with opposition from your ministerial colleagues can be one of the toughest challenges you will face, especially if the formal process for managing these conflicts has broken down. It will not be at all uncommon for you to find other Cabinet ministers objecting to what you are trying to do. Indeed sometimes you will want to object to what they are trying to do. For the most part this is just the normal business of government and many of the issues can be dealt with in ministerial correspondence or thrashed out in a Cabinet Committee. Where they can't there is often no substitute for going round personally to see the colleague who is allegedly about to undermine your entire life's work on fish farming modernisation for fear that it will upset the EU's environmental lobby. When you do manage to get in the same room – and the Tea Room in the House can be a much better place to meet up than in either of your offices surrounded by legions of officials – you will often be pleasantly surprised at how quickly you can find a compromise.

But when none of these methods work you can sometimes find yourself flying without any instruments and with not the slightest sense of where the horizon might be. This was our experience over pension reform in 2006, where we at the DWP and the Prime Minister on one side, and the Chancellor of the Exchequer and the Treasury on the other, were at complete loggerheads over whether pensions should rise in line with earnings as advocated by Lord Turner's Commission or by some other formula. Reaching an agreement was like pulling teeth without any anaesthetic and was only finally resolved in a painful and difficult personal settlement between the two most powerful members of the government. This kind of disagreement is rare but when it happens it can feel like the smooth wheels of government are about to come off altogether. There is never going to be any simple procedure – other than resignation, which was the course taken by Michael Heseltine over the Westland affair and by Clare Short and Robin Cook over Iraq – that can be devised to resolve these kinds of problems. Fortunately they don't happen very often. But when they do only you can decide ultimately the weight to attach to them. The minister whose threats of resignation are so frequent that at No. 10 they are just regarded as part of a normal day – and are filed in the B/F tray while the private office get on with the PM's really important stuff – will rarely be taken very seriously. On the other hand, if you never in your tenure of office reach a point where something matters to you so much that you would consider resigning over it then you may not in the end be doing anything really worthwhile.

So that's it really. Magical tips to handle and overcome all opposition. If only they always worked.

CHAPTER 23

# DATA – HOW NOT TO LOSE IT

*The chapter of knowledge is very short, but the chapter of accidents is a very long one.*

LORD CHESTERFIELD (1694–1773)

FEW SENIOR CIVIL SERVANTS OR ministers who were in place at the time will quickly forget the day in the autumn of 2007 when it came to light that Her Majesty's Revenue and Customs had lost a disc containing the details of some seven million claims to Child Benefit including National Insurance numbers, addresses and bank accounts.

It was little surprise, of course, that the media worked itself up into a righteous indignation of epic proportions.

Newspapers bid to outdo one another in discovering further outrageous examples of lost data and called for more heads to roll in addition to the head of HMRC who had already resigned. And, not to be outdone, the citizens of Britain, or at least some of them, besieged newspapers with their own accounts of misdirected letters, wrongly addressed e-mails and misspelt middle names. Opposition politicians leapt on to the bandwagon, pillorying ministers and the government for their catastrophic incompetence while saying private prayers of thanks that it hadn't happened when they were in office. Only when even they were becoming bored with their own rhetoric did the caravan eventually move on.

But don't worry; we hear you, and those relatively few members of the public who remember all this, say: That was all then. Surely it got sorted out. After all, we're rather good at cleaning up messes even if they shouldn't have happened in the first place. Everyone now loves Terminal 5 at Heathrow; we got the British Library built in the end and CRB checks for teachers are now completed near instantaneously. I've got lots else to do other than worry about data security. And surely that's the Permanent Secretary's job anyway. This can't really be worth a chapter in your book.

Wrong, unfortunately, on almost every count. The situation is better now. Much better. Laptops and memory sticks are encrypted; rules have been tightened; controls put in place; risk registers updated and almost everyone has been trained on how to secure data and prevent its loss. But if you allow yourself to believe that, because all that has been done, the data in your department is now 100 per cent secure, you are making a potentially fatal error. It simply can't be; not if government is going to continue to function. There is simply too much data, being handled by too many people in too many different ways and places, for it ever to be possible to guarantee that data losses are not going to happen. And the very technology that has made so many advances possible has added exponentially to the risks: data that can be e-mailed in vast quantities around the world at the press of a button; memory sticks which you can slip into your pocket – but which can then slip out of it – containing more data on a single stick than the average IBM mainframe could have held twenty years ago; and Blackberries and iPads that allow you to do business all over the world but that can also be lost or stolen in seconds are only some of the risks. Human beings with their limitless capacity to act stupidly or maliciously simply compound them. The truth is that the data in your department is not 100 per cent secure and never can be.

Nor can you simply regard this as the Permanent Secretary's problem while you battle it out with No. 10 to get policy clearance for your hopefully ground-breaking White Paper or polish your party conference speech. Of course it is fundamentally the Permanent Secretary's and the department's responsibility, not yours. And you can take some comfort from the fact that there hasn't (as we go to print) been anything quite as devastating as the child benefit data loss in the intervening seven years since the discs disappeared. In any event, surely no one in their right mind can seriously expect that you can or should take personal responsibility for every file, every e-mail, every laptop and every data stick. That's why we have departmental management after all.

But none of that is going to help you very much on the day when a swathe of sensitive data goes very publicly missing from your department or, worse still, turns up at a council refuse tip in Swindon whereupon a public-spirited citizen promptly hands it over – the payment is incidental; they acted for the good of the country – to whichever Daily they happen to phone first. When that happens it's down to you, and the calls for your blood will make no allowances whatsoever.

So, given that you cannot make this risk completely go way, what can and should you do? Five things.

First, and most important, put this on your own radar screen. Ask the Permanent Secretary to do you a personal note and then take a meeting to discuss it. The mere act of doing so will almost certainly mean that long before the note reaches you the Permanent Secretary will have held at least one and probably several meetings of their own to go through the risks and the issues with their own team. The best Permanent Secretaries will be doing this anyway but, like you, they have a huge number of issues on their plate and they can't make everything a priority. When you hold your meeting ask your civil servants to tell you, completely honestly, what they believe to be the biggest risks and what more they think can be done to reduce them. And then take a follow-up meeting to review the actions that have been taken.

Secondly, recognise that you need someone other than you on the case. So nominate one of your junior ministers to lead for you on this issue. Unless you really think that the issue is going completely by default in the department – in which case you need a very private one-to-one with the Permanent Secretary – make clear that you want them to work absolutely with the Permanent Secretary and that you are looking to them to support the Permanent Secretary's own efforts.

Thirdly, make sure you and your ministers practice what you and the Permanent Secretary are preaching. If your own working practices are so hopelessly insecure as to be the talk of the entire department, then don't expect anyone to take you seriously. So make sure your own laptop and Blackberry are encrypted, don't ask your private office to e-mail classified material to your own completely unprotected PC just to save time, don't read sensitive papers on the train and try really hard to keep hold of your Cabinet papers and not leave them in the airport loo. Remember, too, that today's cameras are entirely capable of taking pictures of the papers you are carrying from 300 yards away and blowing them up perfectly legibly for the front page of tomorrow's newspapers. If you have to carry the papers with you make sure that they are entirely hidden inside the world's most boring file or folder.

Fourthly, ask for this issue to be put regularly on the agenda for the departmental board and ask the Permanent Secretary whether it is being routinely looked at by the department's internal auditors. At the board seek the views and advice of the non-executives and make clear that you would like them to make this one of the issues they keep very much on their radar screen. In other words do everything you sensibly can to keep this at the forefront of people's minds. That won't guarantee that losses will never happen but it will undoubtedly reduce the chances.

Finally, unless you are utterly confident that they are more royalist than the king on this issue, read the riot act personally to your special advisers on the importance of following the department's data security rules. Traditionally, they are some of the worst offenders, regarding almost all of the rules – even if they know that they exist at all – as entirely for the birds. Make clear that it will be their heads on the block as well as yours if they are responsible for a data breach.

OK, do we hear you say once again? So I did all that. What do I do if, despite it all, the worst still happens? Is it survivable?

Well it all depends, of course, on the scale and nature of what goes wrong. If it is really cataclysmic then it may not be. But, even then, much depends on how you and the department react.

Almost certainly you will want to take personal responsibility and to be seen to be doing so. It is terribly tempting in these circumstances to lay publicly into your department – particularly at a time when you are probably furious that this could have happened – and to try to push the responsibility as far away from you as possible. The problem is it rarely works. The world, and certainly the media, is going to hold you responsible – it's your department after all – and will simply add evading responsibility to the charge of gross incompetence. By contrast standing up and accepting responsibility will probably win you some grudging acknowledgement, not least because people will know, deep down, that it is your department that has screwed up and not you personally.

Next, resist the temptation to set out the scale of the problem, and what has happened, until you are absolutely certain of the facts. That is a point of general application, which goes far beyond cases of data loss, but it is true in spades in these circumstances. Most first reports turn out to be wrong both about the scale and nature of the loss and about its cause. The only thing worse than having to tell the House about a major data loss is having to go back to it a second time to admit that your first account was wrong. It may not be comfortable to stick to the line that your first priority is to establish the facts and ensure that individuals are safeguarded but it is undoubtedly preferable to giving an account of events that turns out simply not to be true.

What you can do quickly, however, is to set about reassuring the people whose data has been lost. In the worst cases, like the loss of the Child Benefit data, the papers are likely to be full of the most lurid and bone-chilling predictions of the devastation to people's lives, and their bank accounts, which will most surely follow from whatever has happened. Retired senior police officers – there are a lot of them about and they generally have time on their hands – will be on radio and TV telling how the data is almost certainly already in the hands of the 'Mr Bigs' who are in turn by now selling it on to South American drug traffickers. And the screens will be full of potential victims telling their interviewers of their distress at hearing that their life savings could now be at risk of being wiped out. The fact that in almost no case, including the Child Benefit one, has lost data led actually to any such consequences will most assuredly not feature.

None of this can you stop. But you can make clear that you will indemnify individuals against any losses which they do in fact suffer as a result of the data being lost; you can put out simple advice about how to check your bank and credit card statements for any evidence of identity fraud; and you can open up a helpline for people worried for themselves or their families – though do not do the last of these until you can be sure that there are enough people and lines to handle the calls – you're in enough trouble already.

Finally, it is never a bad idea to call someone high-powered in from outside – a retired Permanent Secretary would naturally be splendid – to urgently review what has happened and to recommend to you the steps that must be taken to avoid a repetition. At the very least that will buy you time and you may well learn something. And you can ask the head of the civil service in parallel – who is almost certainly just as cross about this as you are and is almost certainly reading the riot act to Permanent Secretaries collectively – to advise you on whether, in his view, there are further steps you should take.

If you do all of this and you still get the dreaded phone call from the Chief Whip or the Prime Minister's PPS telling you that, while naturally you still have the PM's complete confidence, it might perhaps be in the party's interest for you to step down just for a while until you can be brought back at the next reshuffle, you can at least console yourself with the thought that it is better than being caught with your own hand in the till. Only your most implacable enemies – by definition, of course, almost always on your own side – will rejoice in your demise.

But actually the chances are that you will see it through. And three months later you will be surprised at how few people remember. As long, of course, as it doesn't happen again!

CHAPTER 24

# FREEDOM OF INFORMATION

*He that increaseth knowledge increaseth sorrow*

KING JAMES BIBLE, ECCLESIASTES 1:18

THIS IS THE ONE OF which you are strongly in favour. Or at least you were. You still have a dog-eared copy somewhere of the Bow Group or Fabian Society pamphlet you co-authored as a student advocating shining a spotlight on the murky corridors of power. And in opposition your researchers regularly bombarded various hapless departments and quangos with FoI requests designed to extract embarrassing and awkward revelations that could go straight into your press release. You still remember the one that finally forced ministers to admit to how few of those sentenced to deportation at the end of their sentences were actually being removed.

But now, suddenly, you're at the receiving end. It's your department which is receiving hundreds of such requests each year asking about things you'd much prefer not to see blazoned over the front pages. It's your grant scheme – the one you announced with such relish to Parliament and on the *Today* programme but which has only managed to make fourteen grants in a year and a half – which is now the subject of the FoI request asking for the release of all your original estimates of likely take-up. Remarkably all this freedom of information stuff is beginning to seem not such a good idea after all, particularly now you're beginning to grasp just how much information your department has in its files.

So what's to do? The first is to at least have the good grace not to berate your private office and your officials every time another potentially embarrassing FoI request turns up in your box. Shooting the messenger has never been the most engaging of ministerial behaviours and in this instance asking your Private Secretary why on earth she personally is expecting you to release the details of the cost overrun on your most high-profile project is probably less than helpful. She isn't. Your government is.

Nor is it a good idea in general to try to suppress information simply because it is embarrassing or awkward. Probably the only thing worse than having to reveal that only fourteen grants have been made in a year and a half against the department's original estimate of 8,000 is the revelation that you and your Spads tried to block releasing the information to such an extent that that itself becomes the story. On the day when that is the front-page lead in *The Guardian* you will almost certainly wish you had simply gritted your teeth and let the information come out when it was originally asked for.

But none of this means that there is nothing sensible, and entirely proper, that you can do. There are a number of things you can and should do as follows.

First, talk to your Permanent Secretary about the department's capability and expertise in this respect. Like any area which has become subject to case law and interpretation, what does, and doesn't, have to be released in response to FoI requests has become increasingly complex in some circumstances. You need to ensure that the department has a team – it doesn't have to be a large one but it has to be good – with real knowledge and understanding in this area. This is not the place to have a series of officials – none of them staying in post for more than six months – trying to pick it up as they go along. On the contrary you, and the Permanent Secretary, need to have some real experts working on the FoI brief who are capable of giving you both seriously expert advice.

Secondly, unless you are really confident of your own knowledge in this area, get yourself given a briefing on the current state of the law and, in particular, those areas where there are exemptions from the general presumption that information requested must be disclosed. Make sure too that the briefing covers the role of the Information Commissioner and the appeal process in cases where you decline to provide the information requested. If possible get your junior ministers and Spads there too. You may find that to have been a very good investment of your time on the day you are faced with the FoI request from hell and you need to know whether you have any legitimate grounds for declining to provide the information requested.

Thirdly, and this one is really important, make sure that the department is operating an effective early-warning system. There are simply going to be times when you are going to have to release information that you know is going to be really difficult to handle. That's unavoidable. What is avoidable is to wake up to a grim news story affecting the department and then to discover that it's based on material which the department has just released in response to an FoI request that you knew nothing about. Make sure that at a very senior level in the department there is a process for looking at all incoming FoI requests and flagging to ministers as soon as they are received the ones that look likely to be contentious or embarrassing. Make sure that one of your Spads is involved in the process and almost certainly at least one of your junior ministers too. That way you can consider before you are hard up against the deadline for release whether there are any legitimate grounds for declining to provide the information being sought. And even if there aren't, it means that you, your press office, and if necessary No. 10, can control at least to some extent the timing of its release and put in place a media-handling plan.

Fourthly, think hard in such cases about what it is that you're going to release. Now that may seem a no-brainer. If someone asks for a fact or a document and there are no legitimate grounds for declining to provide it, you may think that leaves little or no discretion as to what information to provide. That's generally wrong. There will be any number of cases where there is scope for different legitimate interpretations of what is being requested, and hence what to provide in response. And even if there isn't there is scope to add the context even if it's not been asked for. So while you may have to release the original estimate of 8,000 grants being made – against the actual number of fourteen – there is nothing to stop you setting out why the prevailing circumstances have fundamentally changed since that original estimate was made. Depending on the small matter of the actual facts you may even be able to turn the apparent negative into a positive.

Fifthly, on the really difficult requests, don't be reluctant to take advice on your options from both inside and outside the department. Get your top lawyer round your table if you think that will help, ask your officials to consult their counterparts in the Cabinet Office and the Ministry of Justice on whether there are precedents elsewhere in government which may be helpful and, in the final analysis, raise this yourself at the political level with colleagues and No. 10. At the very least that will ensure that they in turn are not taken by surprise on the day that the information you have released leads the evening news. But it may well be that they can suggest legitimate arguments for not disclosing some or all of the information, based on precedent elsewhere, that aren't immediately apparent to your own department.

There is one more longer-term consideration that you may well want to think about. Information can only be released where it exists. That begs the question of how much you want written down in some cases. You can always be given an estimate or briefed on an issue orally. You don't have to ask for it on paper. There is no doubt that one of the less desirable consequences of FoI – to set against all of its undoubted benefits – is that it has already had the effect of causing less government to happen on paper and more simply in discussion round the table. That is not necessarily a good thing. It often makes for less well-considered decision-making and certainly makes it harder to discover subsequently who decided what and on what basis. Historians in fifty years' time may not thank the enthusiasts for open government when they are trying to piece together what happened and why. But, whatever you may think of that on a deeply philosophical basis, it is certainly worth keeping this consideration in mind, particularly when you are dealing with obviously difficult issues. At the very least it suggests that great care needs to be taken over what is said in papers and how meetings and decisions are recorded. There will be enough FoI goals scored against you without adding lots of goals of your own to the score sheet.

There are many and various views both within government and outside on whether the introduction of Freedom of Information has been a positive or a negative overall for the business of government. Despite some of its probably unintended consequences, which undoubtedly include a chilling effect on civil servants writing their advice as plainly as they once did, we both believe that greater transparency about how government is conducted is, in the end, in the public interest and a considerable safeguard against the abuse of power. In the final analysis, save in rare cases, hidden government is bad government. But that doesn't mean that, as a minister, while remaining true to that belief, you cannot take sensible steps of the kind we have set out here to make the consequences of FoI for your department more controlled and effective.

And on the day when all else fails, and you are plastered all over the media as a result of the information you have been obliged to release – as well as remembering that in three months' time almost no one will remember what all the fuss was about – you can at least go back to the pamphlet you wrote to recall why you thought this was such a good thing. And on the even later day, if it ever comes, when you find yourself back in opposition, you can happily set your researchers to work once again to come up with the FoI requests that will send the ultimate chill down the spine of your successor.

CHAPTER 25

# IT'S TIME TO GO

*Things do not change; we change.*

HENRY THOREAU (1817–1862)

YOU'RE READING THIS, PROBABLY, NOT long after you've arrived and already there's a section on the time to go. 'Thank you very much,' you may well say, 'if it's all the same to you I'll decide when it's time to go; and I'll decide without any advice from an ex-minister, still less from an ex-mandarin sitting on a bloated index-linked pension drinking gin and tonics in Surbiton.' Fair enough, it's Watford actually and the ex-mandarin doesn't do gin and tonics. But we get the message.

Nevertheless, just to persist. As Enoch Powell did famously say, 'all political careers end in failure'. But there are certainly degrees of failure and, as we point out in our advice on 'Resignation', there are many different ways of going; some a lot better and some a lot worse. What is undoubtedly true is that all political careers have a beginning, a middle and an end; and you may want to give some thought now as to how, ideally, you might want yours to end. That won't guarantee that it will work out like that but having some kind of a plan, if only in your head, will at least give you some bearings as your career goes forward.

The first question to ask yourself – really ask yourself – is whether you can envisage any other life than that of a politician. If the truthful answer is 'no' – and it is a perfectly honourable answer – then you are pretty well committed to staying on the political roller coaster until something – fate, losing your seat, scandal if you're very silly or very unlucky or just plain old age – throws you off. If that is the case don't spend too much time worrying now about when might be the right time to go because the truth is that you're never going to want to. So get on, do your best, read the other chapters of our book and try to enjoy it. It's the life you want after all.

If, on the other hand, you can seriously envisage a life after politics, read on.

When you first enter politics, when you first get selected for a seat, when you first win an election and enter the House, when you are first made a minister no matter in how obscure a department, when you first speak from the despatch box, when you first enter the Cabinet (if indeed you do), all of these are great moments which you almost certainly deserve, and deserve to enjoy. As we have said earlier in our book, ignore all the cynicism about politics and politicians; if we didn't have people willing and able to pursue political careers we would not have a democracy. And what's more you do, as our earlier chapter says, have a real chance to make a difference. You may very well already have done so; if not, now's your chance and you'll probably never get a better one.

The problem, if there is one, comes later. There is no doubt that political life and, above all, ministerial office exacts a very considerable toll. A very senior business executive once told one of us that she thought there were only so many flights across the Atlantic that any human being could withstand. It may be, similarly, that there are only so many debates, so many elections, so many ministerial boxes, so many impossible issues, so many civil servants bearing advice and so many constituency engagements that any minister can withstand before they start to lose their edge and their energy. And there may be only so many days, nights and weeks away from one's partner and family that any relationship can ultimately endure.

Now there are no hard-and-fast rules in this respect, and certainly no universal truths of a Jane Austen kind. We have both met, and worked for and with, ministers whose edge and energy, to say nothing of their passion and conviction, was as strong towards the end of their political lives as at the beginning, indeed in some cases stronger. But we have also seen a number – good men and women without exception – who were clearly becoming ground down by the sheer weight and relentless pressure of ministerial office, and who were clearly in danger of simply being on a treadmill they did not know how to get off. For some electoral defeat actually came as a relief, a way of getting off the treadmill without having openly to step down or opt out.

So if indeed that scenario is one that you can both identify with but want to avoid, it may be worth consciously putting some limits into your own perspective – so many Parliaments, so many general elections, so many years an MP – that you would want to form the outer limits of your political life. Of course doing that doesn't mean that they will ever bite, and you may never tell anyone else that such limits even exist in your mind let alone what they are, but they may at least help you to navigate your career, and keep your sanity, once all those truly remarkable first political experiences are behind you.

Ann Widdecombe – not a politician anyone would ever have accused of lacking passion or conviction – describes in her autobiography *Strictly Ann* how at a certain point in her career she found herself tiring not of politics but of the political game. She tells how, in the run-up to the 2005 general election, she decided that, if re-elected, it would be her last Parliament, and how she rejected the advice of those who advised her not to say so publicly for fear of people thinking that she might be losing interest. While glad that she had spent her life as she had, she had simply concluded it was time for a change.

Of course it's easier to change if you know what you want to change to. In Ann Widdecombe's case she had already embarked on a second career as a novelist and that was long before her celebrated appearance on *Strictly Come Dancing*. It is certainly easier to contemplate a second career if you have one either to hand or in prospect. So – despite all of the pressures of ministerial life – it is almost certainly worth trying to keep your other interests and experience alive. The ex-minister amongst the two of us somehow managed to find the time while in office to write a history of his local regiment during World War One. That may be at the outer limits of the possible. But still doing something that appeals to you away from the political world has a great deal to commend it. Apart from anything else it gives you a better excuse when your Private Secretary enquires rather plaintively why, for the third time that week, you have brought back your ministerial box untouched into the department.

So that's it; the one serious piece of advice in this chapter, unless you are simply a political obsessive for whom no other world will ever hold any attraction, is to keep in mind that one day you may indeed want to go, and to have at least in your head a plan for when that day might be. You will by then, hopefully, have had a successful ministerial career and left some real mark behind you. When your successors idly look at your photo on the wall along with those of all your predecessors they may well remember some of what you achieved. And in the meantime you can always begin in your spare time to write the novel you've always had inside you. Good luck!

CHAPTER 26

# RESIGNATION

*I want to get out with my greatness intact.*

MUHAMMAD ALI, 1974

AND SO TO THE FINAL chapter of Part I of our book, written fittingly – it's about how to leave your life as a minister after all – by John.

All ministerial careers come to an end and yours will be no exception. You may not want to think much about this at the start of your time in office but at some point you need to give the manner of your departure some serious consideration. After all, it may be one of the most important things you are remembered for so it is a good idea to spend some time planning how you are going to behave when this moment in your political life arrives, as it inevitably will. It comes as a perpetual surprise that so many ministers seem totally unprepared for it when it actually happens.

For some, the lucky ones, the end of your ministerial career will come as the result of a general election defeat. This is by far and away the best way to leave government. You all leave together at exactly the same time. There is indeed such a thing as safety in numbers. All the focus will in any case be on the outgoing Prime Minister and what he says and does. There will be very little attention or interest given to the departure of Cabinet or junior ministers. In the mass exodus from office that follows an election defeat there will be many more interesting stories about the new government and its ministers for the media to concern themselves with. You, however, will be history, at least for the moment. Hopefully, your place in it will at least be secure for now.

On the dissolution of Parliament you will almost certainly have said goodbye to your senior team of officials and advisers because, as a seasoned political operator, you will have had a pretty good idea of whether your party is going to be returned to office or not. Take your leave quietly, with as good grace and as little fanfare as possible. And if you genuinely want to thank the people who have worked so hard for you – as you should – then this is probably the best time to do it – there won't be much opportunity to do so after the election results are in. By then you will be in your constituency and your successor will be very quickly installed in your old department. As recent events have shown, it is wise to resist the temptation to leave your successor a note, particularly one that attempts to be humorous. It will almost certainly backfire and you can be left looking foolish and flippant – the very things you were anxious to avoid while you were a minister. If you are fortunate enough to have been re-elected to the House of Commons then you will be able to share any private thoughts you might have about your department with the new Secretary of State. Some things, after all, are better done in private, even in the age of freedom of information.

If you are not going as a result of a general election but rather are resigning at a time of your own choosing, that should mean that you have given considerable thought to why you are going and what you intend to say about your departure. In my case I told the Prime Minister weeks before the reshuffle that I intended to stand down from the Cabinet for personal reasons. I was not going to contest the 2010 general election and wanted to pursue a different direction in my life. I was able to go on my own terms, hopefully without causing the government any more political difficulty (by then it had managed to generate quite enough of its own) even though I was deeply reluctant to leave a department I had always wanted to lead. When Alan Milburn resigned as Health Secretary in 2003 he created a positive story both around his departure from high office, which was for very genuine personal reasons to do with his young family, as well as the expectation that he would surely return at some point to a very senior Cabinet position. In these circumstances resignation does not have to mark the end of a career, but only the beginning of a different phase to it, and does not have to harm the government at all.

Being sacked is, however, an altogether more difficult situation. In these circumstances anger and frustration at your misfortune and the obvious mistake the Prime Minister is making can easily get the better of you. And that may only be magnified when you learn who your replacement is going to be, which may well seem the final straw. But context is, once again, everything. If your departure from government has come about during a wider Cabinet or ministerial reshuffle then there is probably still scope to go with a modicum of good grace and at least some praise ringing in your ears, even if the truth is that you are being let go because of dissatisfaction with the way you have been running your department. Hopefully, however unfair you may have thought it, this sense of dissatisfaction will not have come as a total surprise. Your parliamentary colleagues will have been speaking to the Whips and, if the system is working properly, these concerns will have found their way back to you. Poor performances in the media or in Parliament itself should have set your own political alarm bells ringing.

The good news, however, is that even in these cases there is a protocol to follow. It starts with a call from the PM in advance of the reshuffle. You may or may not be expecting the bad news but you will be able at least to agree some words which will be used to describe the contribution you have made to the government. You will usually be offered the opportunity to offer your own resignation, making it seem as though it is you who has decided on the timing of your departure, rather than the PM. You may still be shocked at losing your job but the process will at least allow you to create a softer landing for yourself than would otherwise have been the case. Prime Ministers, after all, need to refresh their governments from time to time. Restless backbenchers have to be brought into the warm embrace of government (and become bound by ministerial responsibility) and good ministers have to be promoted. The equation can only be balanced if others are let go. This iron law of politics will be cold comfort to you but being able to manage a dignified exit in such circumstances is immensely preferable to the other alternative – of being booted out unceremoniously. And remember, these will be the only two options in front of you.

There are a number of things to consider in this respect – not least the possibility of an eventual return to government at some point in the future as well as your post-ministerial career in politics. History is littered with the burning wreckage of embittered former ministers whose view of the world has been rendered toxic as the result of their enforced departure from government. This sense of entitlement to ministerial office – 'who the hell does the Prime Minister think he is?' – represents a profound misunderstanding of the nature of ministerial life and always reflects badly on those who carry this lonely torch of wounded pride. And if you do decide to do the martyred minister act don't expect the backbenches to be behind you. They won't be. Very few, if any, of your colleagues will travel this journey at your side. It is in fact the fast-track route to disaffection and alienation from your party and colleagues. For most people, it should be the way of going to be avoided at all costs. And remember, your departure will create new opportunities for others and this too will condition the behaviour of many of your parliamentary colleagues. There is nothing like the smell of ministerial advancement to keep troublemakers inside the tent.

It follows that it is usually a good idea to wait a while after the news of your departure from government has been announced and choreographed before saying anything you might regret, even though you may be bursting to shout from the rooftops about how unfair everything is. Strangely enough, the country will somehow be finding a way to carry on without you, however inconceivable that may seem. The truth is that your party has many other talented people in it beside you. Thank goodness for that.

Being sacked or resigning outside of any wider reshuffle is an altogether different proposition, as here you will be the entire focus of the story. What you say and do will be forensically crawled over by every pundit and commentator. In these circumstances a whirlwind can quickly gather pace around you, making rational thought extremely difficult. Finding yourself under a frenzy of media pressure to resign for something you have done or a mistake you have made – either in your private life or as a minister – is one of those car-crash moments which by definition is almost impossible to prepare for. As a politician one of your fundamental skills is to know when you need simply to apologise – and to accept the consequences – and when you should carry on defending yourself and your behaviour. The trouble is that very often there is an all too predictable pattern with an all too predictable outcome. Your first instinct, particularly if you think you have the backing of No. 10, is to do everything possible to hang on and hope the story will eventually go away. But the reality is that it rarely does. If a story has a bad smell it will linger. Even when a story lacks real substance – as it did in Andrew Mitchell's case – a story can gather momentum which simply becomes unstoppable. Perception can sometimes count more than the facts.

It is essential therefore to take advice when the story first breaks – and you will generally have some warning that it is about to – from the people you trust the most, both in your political circles but also outside, amongst your family, friends and advisers. Remember too that others get a say on this as well. No. 10 will follow very carefully any threat to the reputation and good name of the government as a whole. You will need to keep close to this source of counsel as well as to the Whips' Office. The worst outcome of all is the forced resignation after weeks of denials and stubborn refusal to acknowledge what has become obvious to everybody else – that you will have to go. Timing is therefore critical and your own judgement is central to this.

In particular you need to consider the resignation option right at the start of trouble brewing up and be clear about whether you want to exercise it. All your instincts, of course, will be to avoid giving the media a scalp and possibly damaging the government in the process. And you may well feel that you are being treated incredibly unfairly. But an early lancing of the boil can not only help the government recover its position rather than hinder it, but also makes much more possible your own eventual return to office at some point in the future. The resignation in early 2014 of Mark Harper as Immigration Minister is a good example after he found out that his cleaner did not have permission to work in the UK. Rather than trying to tough it out he chose to resign straightaway and emerged with his integrity intact and the issue immediately closed down. The same was true in the case of the swift resignation of David Laws in May 2010 after only two weeks as Chief Secretary to the Treasury, but who has subsequently been reappointed a minister. Resignation in such circumstances can be seen as a principled action and something which does not spell the end of a politician's ministerial career, indeed Mark Harper has already been reappointed as a minister. The key here is quick action. You need to fall on your own sword, not be forced onto it because of a media campaign. Parliament and political parties can be forgiving to those who go voluntarily, but are rarely so when a resignation is dragged from a reluctant victim. In these cases there is rarely ever a route back to office.

The final form of resignation – on a matter of principle – is a rare event in our politics. This is not because politicians have no principles, but because many misjudge the moment and hang on for months or maybe even years in the hope that their views may eventually prevail. But the sense that they should have gone earlier will sometimes haunt them and entirely overshadow their own and other people's view of their ministerial careers.

Genuine political resignations – by which I mean those cases where a minister resigns because of a fundamental political difference with the direction of government policy – are becoming extremely rare. This is largely the result of the remorseless rise of machine politics and the discipline of remaining 'on message'. However, when these sorts of divergence do emerge, a minister is deliberately putting themselves on a different trajectory to that being offered by the Prime Minister and the Cabinet. Here there are no rules to follow other than your own political instincts – your sense of what is the right thing to do. When James Purnell, for example, resigned as Secretary of State for Work and Pensions in 2009 he did so because he genuinely believed that the government needed a different Prime Minister to lead it to victory in the upcoming general election. It was an individual decision taken without the knowledge or support of any of his closest political friends, and I counted myself as one of them. James had been a junior minister in my department when I had served at DWP and had made a huge and positive impact on the department. As my fellow author will confirm, he was liked and respected in equal measure by his civil servants, something that sadly cannot be said about every minister. He and I shared a similar view of Labour politics. His resignation did not result in any change of direction or leadership in the government. But neither in the same token did it harm him as a politician. Quite the opposite. While he was condemned by a few of his colleagues, the overwhelming reaction was respect for the openness and honesty of his decision. The same was true when Robin Cook, Clare Short, John Denham and Philip Hunt resigned from the government over the war in Iraq in 2003. In my view, our politics are better served when people behave in this way. Honesty in politics can never do a politician or minister any lasting damage. It is dishonesty that is ultimately far more corrosive to both politics and politicians.

# PART II

## LESSONS LEARNED

Welcome to Part II of the book.

Part I has, hopefully, enabled you to be the perfect Secretary of State and other readers to gain some insight into the real life of a minister.

Part II is different. We want to use it to distil some of our own thoughts gained from our time in government about what we learned and what we think might be done differently. It is not intended as a treatise on government and there is much that it does not cover. But we hope it may make some contribution to the current debate on how the government of this country should be structured and carried out in the future. Whatever party we happen to support, we must surely all have an interest in the business of government being carried out as effectively as possible.

CHAPTER 27

# WHAT WORKS

IT IS CUSTOMARY IN ALL government White and Green Papers on anything to do with government or the civil service to include at the outset a throat-clearing paragraph or two to the effect that we remain, in many respects, the envy of the world in terms of our system of government. The true translation of such paragraphs is normally that, at least in the view of those putting forward the paper's proposals for change, their level of frustration with the 'machine' has now reached so high a level that they have concluded that the time for fundamental change has come. By contrast, before putting forward our own proposals for change, we want to signal some areas where we genuinely believe on the basis of our own experience in government that the machine is not fundamentally broken and, accordingly, does not need wholesale fixing.

CHAPTER 28

# HONESTY AND INTEGRITY

NOTHING IS NOW MORE FASHIONABLE than to decry the honesty and integrity of politicians and, only to a slightly lesser extent, those who support them, be they in the civil service, political parties or elsewhere. The MPs' expenses scandal was simply the final proof to many that politicians as a whole are venal, self-seeking, mendacious and corrupt. Media coverage tends continually to reinforce this view, whether it is the bear pit of Prime Minister's Question Time, the classic blood-curdling *Today* programme interview or the call for heads to roll as soon as anything anywhere in government goes awry. Even estate agents and bankers gain higher ratings in polls of public trust than politicians.

The only problem with this robustly held and near universal

view is that it is near universally wrong. There are corrupt and deceitful politicians; there are corrupt and deceitful civil servants; there are corrupt and deceitful 'advisers' and lobbyists. But they are in a tiny minority. In our experience the vast majority of politicians and ministers – irrespective of party – the vast majority of civil servants and the vast majority of those otherwise engaged in politics are not only honest but also, by their own lights, seeking to do their best in whatever role they are in. After, between us, more than half a century in government we can both count on the fingers of one hand the exceptions to this rule (and no, we're not naming names).

Does it matter that truth and perception in this respect are so far apart and, even if it does, can anything be done about it? We think it does matter in that it is the perception that drives so much of the deep-rooted public distrust of politics and politicians and which undoubtedly causes some very talented people either to decide never to enter politics in the first place or to decide to leave it in the face of such relentless and overwhelming hostility. In a cynical age the cynics are in general allowed to proceed unencumbered by the facts.

The much more difficult question is whether anything can be done or whether, rather like the weather, this perception of politics and politicians will simply always be with us. Remember that even those great politicians of yesteryear – George Washington, Winston Churchill, Konrad Adenauer – were often subject to vitriolic criticism and abuse at the time when they held office. Only the perspective of history has led the world to view them in a different light.

We think it idle to believe that anything in this respect is going to change any time soon; the cynicism and the hostility is simply too entrenched and deep-rooted for that. But we think that should not be a reason for supine acquiescence in the perpetuation of what is largely a myth. We think that politicians, civil servants, academics and commentators who share our view should be more willing to take on the cynics and the stereotypes. In our own way we do so by airing this issue here.

CHAPTER 29

# A POLITICALLY IMPARTIAL CIVIL SERVICE

IN RECENT YEARS THE FUNDAMENTAL concept – which had existed largely unchallenged since the famous Northcote–Trevelyan report was published in 1854 – of a politically neutral civil service serving, in the famous words repeated to all new civil servants, 'the government of the day', has come increasingly under question. This near uniquely British concept has been contrasted with the alternatives in both the United States and most of Western Europe where the higher echelons of the civil service are political in the sense either that their incumbents arrive and leave with their political masters or that their own political affiliations are publicly known and acknowledged. By contrast only one of the joint authors of this book knows how the other votes.

Those advocating a move to something closer to the American or mainstream European model argue that it would remove a huge cause of the frustration of successive ministers if they knew, without question, that those in the most important positions immediately surrounding them were their political supporters. They contrast this with what they see either as the inbuilt caution or, worse, downright obstructionism that they associate with some if not all of those in the senior civil service. Many holding this view also believe that allowing ministers to appoint their own top teams – the latest variant of this formula being the current government's proposal to introduce what they term 'extended ministerial offices' – would allow them to bring in the most talented people whoever they were, rather than having to accept those they happen to inherit in the civil service.

These are powerful arguments and they should not be dismissed lightly. In particular, we believe, and propose later in this chapter, that ministers should be free to bring in acknowledged experts in the areas of most importance to them without in every case having to go through the current civil service rules of 'free and open competition'. We also believe that there is a case for relaxing the current restrictions on the number of special advisers whom a minister can appoint to reflect something more of the reality of the huge and complex departments over which many of them preside. Not all special advisers have had the best press in recent years and the behaviours of a small minority have overstepped acceptable bounds; but overall they have been a powerful force for good in government rather than the reverse.

But none of this is to say that we would want to throw the baby out with the bathwater and move away from a fundamentally politically neutral civil service willing, in those famous words, 'to speak truth unto power'. The best ministers that we have seen, and we have seen many, have clearly benefited from the objectivity and challenge of their senior civil servants. In our experience the best policy does not in general emerge from the already persuaded persuading the already persuaded. Nor does it emerge from an absence of corporate memory and an unwillingness to ask the hard questions about practicality and resources. Many of those who have complained loudest about the constraints supposedly imposed by their civil servants have been weak ministers with poor policies. Using their civil servants as whipping boys has been a convenient excuse to hide their own inadequacies. By contrast, clear and determined ministers have in general found that they have received strong support from the civil service teams around them.

The other powerful argument for a politically neutral civil service is the degree to which it facilitates a swift transition of power which enables an incoming government to hit the ground running. Contrast the two furniture vans at No. 10 – one at the front door and one at the back – which characterise the incredibly fast handover of power following the defeat of an incumbent Prime Minister at a general election in the UK with the months – sometimes a year or more – that it takes Washington to put a new administration in place following a change of President. Would politicians here willingly sacrifice this advantage? And, of course, if a major crisis – national or international – straddles the transition, the in-coming government is deprived of the knowledge and understanding of the senior officials who have dealt with the crisis on behalf of the outgoing administration.

We do believe, as we set out later, that the Whitehall policy process should be opened up much more widely than it is currently and we certainly believe that not only public servants should deliver public policies. But we also believe that, overall, the UK has been well served, and continues to be well served, by a politically neutral civil service which works, without hesitation, for the government of the day but which is also able and unafraid to challenge that government where it believes that its policies are insufficiently thought through or robust. And we believe that we need to be vigilant against covert politicisation of the civil service whereby some civil servants may begin to believe that they need to be on the same political wavelength as ministers in order to get on and some ministers begin to believe that that is something which they are entitled to expect. This would in our view not be a sensible path to follow.

CHAPTER 30

# PUBLIC SERVICE DELIVERY

IT HAS BECOME ALMOST A commonplace in recent years to accept that anything delivered by the public sector is by definition inefficient, sub-standard and unimaginative while, by contrast, the private sector is vastly more efficient, cost conscious and innovative. Successive governments have turned to the private sector for advice and inspiration on how to beef up delivery, ginger up the hapless public servants currently doing the job and explain how it – whatever 'it' is from providing back-office services for the police to running care homes for the elderly – could undoubtedly be better run by a commercial organisation.

And sometimes it's true. There are many – far too many – poor-quality public services being delivered by managers who are at best well-meaning and at worst uncaring. No one hearing the case a year or so back of the patient who in desperation rang 999 from his hospital bed to try and get a drink of water, or reading the Public Accounts Committee's report into the fiasco at the Rural Payments Agency, can believe other than that these were public services and public service managers of whom we should be thoroughly ashamed. And no one seeing the best of which the private sector is capable – bringing imaginative new products to market and delivering at times superb consumer choice – can believe other than that there must be many services which would be far better being delivered by the private sector.

The problem is that for each such example there is a counter-example. There are also first-rate public services ranging from the incredibly slick vehicle licensing operation at DVLA to what we both believe was one of the best examples of hugely improved public service delivery at Jobcentre Plus. And for every example of great private sector delivery there are others – ranging from the banking debacles which have left us all with mountains of debt to the abject failure of G4S to provide sufficient security guards for the Olympics – which have caused every bit as much grief as any failures in the public sector. No wonder that the various private sector gurus regularly brought into government by successive Prime Ministers and Chancellors are viewed somewhat sceptically by those inside government who are supposed to sit at their feet and learn.

At the risk of it sounding trite and self-evident, our own view is that who is best placed to deliver a particular public service should be a pragmatic not a theological question. There will be many occasions when that indeed will be the private, or indeed the third, sector. That is particularly the case where first-rate delivery is going to require large-scale, up-front investment – something with which government invariably struggles – or involve taking and retaining substantial risk, which government is rarely best placed to do. Nor is government generally in its element delivering large-scale back-office processes where the economies of scale will always tend to favour the private sector.

On the other hand, the direct delivery of face-to-face services to the citizen – whether social services or driving tests – may carry greater public acceptance if not seen as directly linked to commercial considerations. And areas where those delivering services are required to exercise law enforcement powers – be they at the border or on the streets – may be harder to reconcile with private sector delivery.

But even here there are counter-examples; privately run prisons delivering vast improvements in their treatment of prisoners on the one hand; publicly run job-broking services out-performing their private sector competitors on the other. Which brings us back to where we began; this should be a pragmatic, evidence-based choice not an ideological battleground. And with recognition that, in the end, a mixed economy delivery system is likely to perform better overall than either a wholly private or a wholly public one. Poor performance in any part of the public sector cannot be allowed to go unchallenged and we should not shrink from taking whatever measures are necessary in order to provide the public with the high-quality services they increasingly demand and expect from government. Contestability is the key issue here.

That is why we both believe in this context that it is the absence of monopoly that works rather than the private or the public sector being inherently better. There is no doubt that one of the spurs for greatly improved delivery in many areas of our public services in recent years has been the prospect or threat – use whatever word you will – of contestability or privatisation. Nothing engenders complacency more than a belief on the part of an existing service provider that they will be delivering that service for evermore. Nothing stimulates change and innovation more than the threat of losing that service. Of course, for this to be truly effective, it needs to be a two-way street. Just as there must be a prospect of services being transferred from public to private provision, so there must also be a real prospect of the reverse transfer happening where a private sector provider fails spectacularly to deliver. There have already been examples of that – Network Rail taking over from Railtrack for example – and there may well need to be more in the future.

But if these are examples of areas where we think that what we already have has considerable merit there are others where, in the light of our joint experience, we would advocate more fundamental change.

CHAPTER 31

# MANAGING CHANGE

As is evident at any airport bookshop this is a subject on which more books have been written than most of us have had hot dinners. Arguably there are very few organisations that manage change well – perhaps more people should buy the books – but it is our experience that, in general, change is managed even more poorly inside government than elsewhere. If that is indeed so, there are a number of possible explanations for it. One is that government – even by the standards of the ever more quickly changing society in which it operates – is particularly given to focusing on the short-term. Another is that very few senior civil servants, let alone ministers, have any real experience or understanding of change management. And a third is that government continually under-values and under-rewards the skills necessary to deliver real and lasting change successfully. But whatever the underlying causes the fact is, as the Public Accounts Committee has repeatedly demonstrated, that change management in government is far too often poor.

So what can be done? There is no magic bullet but we have six suggestions to offer:

First, there should be a conscious determination to keep ministers and civil servants in post for longer. Almost all major change requires long-term commitment. Nothing is more certain to increase the chances of failure in the delivery of major projects than for there to be perpetual movement amongst the key players, be they ministers, civil servants or professional advisers. The last government, at least as far as ministers were concerned, not only ignored this principle but turned ministerial reshuffles into an Olympic sport; the DWP in the five years running up to the last election had five different Secretaries of State, six employment ministers and seven pensions ministers. None of that was particularly unusual in Whitehall. The present Prime Minister, to his credit, has resisted the temptation to engage in frequent major reshuffles with the result that some ministers are now in their fourth year in post and have thus become genuinely expert about their subject areas. Nor is the phenomenon of perpetual motion confined to ministers. Indeed, with the increased length of ministerial tenure under the current administration, it is ministers who are now complaining of their perpetually changing civil servants rather more than the other way round. Senior civil servants, for a variety of reasons, move far more frequently between posts than is desirable. The result, all too often, is not only a serious lack of continuity and experience but also frequent changes of direction and emphasis as each new player, minister or civil servant, brings in new priorities and wishes. None of this can be totally prevented; ministers resign, civil servants are promoted, events happen. But a clear determination to extend the length of all key ministerial and civil service appointments would do much to increase the chances of success in delivering major change.

Secondly, ministers should be appointed to posts at least in part on the basis that they have the skills and experience needed for the post in question. In no other serious occupation or profession would that be the last consideration ever taken into account at the point when appointments to senior positions are made. But it is in politics. Now this is not straightforward. A Prime Minister appointing their ministerial team is always going to be balancing lots of different factors with only limited room for manoeuvre. But there have nevertheless been some spectacularly inept appointments in recent times (you can ask but our lips are sealed) when alternatives were available. At least as a starting point we believe that relevant knowledge and experience should be an explicit consideration in making ministerial appointments. It would in that context concentrate the mind, even perhaps of a Prime Minister, if the Public Administration Select Committee were to be given the role in assessing, after each major round of ministerial appointments, the degree to which they believed such considerations had been taken into account.

Thirdly, ministers, and senior civil servants, going into posts with direct responsibility for, or oversight of, major change programmes or projects should have to undergo specific training in the disciplines involved. Another of the near Alice in Wonderland fantasies of our political life is that on the day a new Secretary of State, or Permanent Secretary, is appointed they are miraculously assumed to have all the skills they need to lead their department. The reality is often closer to the precise opposite. None of this reflects badly on the individuals in question. Particularly as far as ministers are concerned it is simply a fact of our political system that many come into government having had little or no real-world experience outside of politics. For senior civil servants there is less excuse but the same phenomenon can certainly occur. But that does not mean that we need perpetuate this lack of skills as if it were some kind of badge of honour. It would not be difficult, for example, to run a series of short courses for both ministers and senior civil servants designed to give them at least a basic understanding of the key change and project management disciplines. More fundamentally, it should over time be made a requirement that any civil servant taking on the 'SRO' (Senior Responsible Owner) role for any major project should have to have a specific project management qualification.

Fourthly, and with the same aim in mind, we believe that we need, once and for all, to get away from the concept of the 'gifted amateur' or 'generalist' in the civil service. That may have had its place in a simpler, less technology-driven society where expectations were far lower. And there will always be the need for those at the very top of departments to be able to take a broader view across disciplines. But one consequence of the present government's (relative) success in having ministers in place for longer is that it has shown up how shallow the subject-specific knowledge of some senior civil servants is. Over the years there have been a number of well-intentioned initiatives designed to embed greater discipline and knowledge-specific skills into civil service recruitment and promotion policies. But none has taken serious hold. What we believe to be needed is to move the civil service far more closely towards private sector, and indeed local government, practice in which people are in general recruited, on the basis of their knowledge and expertise, into specific disciplines and roles in which they will be expected to stay for a substantial period. Some of that has been happening in some departments but it is still very far from being the norm.

Fifthly, and intrinsically linked to the previous point, we should be prepared to pay what it takes to get the right people in place to deliver major change. Nothing is more toxic currently than the subject of pay for senior public servants. Any salary in six figures is by definition not only hideous extravagance but also, in the view of much of our media, an affront to decent hard-working taxpayers. And the ultimate crime is for anyone to be paid more than the Prime Minister – one of the most irrational measures ever to be adopted by a government but nonetheless now remarkably potent in its application. In the real world, of course, senior public servants are never going to be paid at the same level as their counterparts in private industry and nor should they be. But we need to be prepared to pay enough to attract and retain the quality of person needed to deliver successfully. And we need to measure their value not primarily in terms of what they cost but of what they deliver. Just as we both believe that the present government deserves congratulation for trying to slow the ministerial merry-go-round, so we both believe that it deserves criticism for playing so blatantly to the gallery on public sector pay.

Finally, and perhaps most importantly, we need to have the confidence as a society to take, and keep to, long-term decisions. Setting up and dismantling an entire government department within two years for example – the late and unlamented Department for Innovation, Universities and Skills – would take almost any award for how not to do government. But setting up and then dismantling the Border Agency before the ink on its letterhead was dry would come a close second. Sadly, other such examples abound. Governments being prepared to take and stick to tough long-term decisions – and at times being prepared to work with parties in opposition to gain consensus and thus increase the chances of continuity across an election – may never be the greatest sound bite but it has the potential to pay huge dividends in the long term. And there are some areas, such as pension reform, where this has been shown to be possible. We commend it to our readers.

CHAPTER 32

# OPENING UP GOVERNMENT

COMPARED TO WHEN WE BOTH entered government – one of us further back than the other it has to be said – government today is vastly more open to the outside world than ever it was. The advent of special advisers, 'Goats' (though see our chapters on them in Part I), and individuals called in to undertake specific enquiries or pieces of work has already opened up the range of support and advice available to ministers. All of these changes have brought benefits. It is also much more normal now for ministers to meet regularly with think tanks, pressure groups and a wide variety of community and other organisations. Within the civil service it is now much more the norm to open up senior roles to external appointment and to bring in talented individuals from outside. The

DWP top team in the five years up to the last election was split almost equally between career civil servants and external appointees in a way that would have been unimaginable a generation before.

And yet sitting within it Whitehall can still feel very much like a closed shop. Part of that is simply the physical layout of the typical government department. Normally on the top floor of whatever is its headquarters building – the views tend to be better there than in the basement – are clustered together the offices of its Secretary of State and other ministers, the Permanent Secretary, the special advisers and their private offices. Ministers spend a large part of their lives in these few hundred square metres as, on a typical day, a succession of 'officials' – the rather arcane name still used throughout Whitehall to describe the department's civil servants – and outside visitors are wheeled into their offices for meetings. Even when they leave the building it tends to be cocooned in their ministerial car which hastens, after their excursion to wherever it might be, to bring them back as quickly as possible to the safety of the mother ship.

It is little surprise that this tends to reinforce the much talked about 'silo government'. It is not just, or even primarily, the opposition who tend to become the enemy in such an environment. Other government departments come to be seen almost in the same light. Outsiders become interest groups to be managed rather than the holders of views to be welcomed. Even No. 10 – not to mention No. 11 – can come to be seen as part of this largely hostile outside world.

Is there an alternative? As we noted in Part I of the book, in New Zealand – a far-away country of which we know little but always a rather intriguing one to UK politicians – ministers have their offices together in the capital, Wellington, in a separate building (known to everyone as the 'Beehive' in recognition of its external appearance) away from their departments. Ministers from New Zealand say that this makes for a more genuinely collegiate government with less in-fighting between departments. That may, of course, be as much a function of a country whose entire population is only around half that of London but it is an interesting demonstration, nevertheless, that there are other ways of locating government. We think that it would at least be worth the government commissioning a serious piece of research on the New Zealand experience, designed to establish whether it might be worth following here.

But probably much more important than their physical location are the sources from which ministers draw their advice and ideas. Overwhelmingly, still, policy advice to ministers comes from their civil servants, for the most part still written down in long hard-copy submissions which fill their ministerial boxes every evening. It is a way of doing business that, in truth, has changed little in its fundamentals for the last half-century at least.

And it has its advantages. The best policy civil servants in Whitehall are very, very good: clever, experienced and knowledgeable. Just because they've seen a lot of it before does not mean that they cannot be imaginative and energetic. Unlike many of those sitting outside of government they do not in general have any vested interest in the advice they offer. And while writing that advice down can make for excruciatingly long and tedious submissions, there is nothing quite like the discipline of having to commit arguments to paper for causing their authors to have to think through what it is they are actually advising.

But there is another side to all this too. While the notion of the 'gifted amateur' is no longer as fashionable as it once was in Whitehall, it remains the case – as we have noted above – that many of those providing advice to ministers have no more detailed or specialist knowledge of their subject area, and sometimes less, than the ministers whom they are supposedly advising. And, despite efforts to change the culture in some departments, there is still an expectation that the best and the brightest will move regularly from post to post in search of career advancement, with many of them looking to move on an almost annual basis. It is little wonder that some ministers come to think that their needs and wishes are at the bottom of the priority list when their civil servants are deciding who goes where.

And the other side of the 'there are some brilliant people in Whitehall' coin is that there are still too many who are risk averse, conservative and time serving. This is less a question of 'them having their own agenda', as some ministers are still at times wont to suspect, as of their having an agenda of simply keeping their heads down and hoping that ideas for more radical change will simply go away. Nothing is more frustrating, whether as Permanent Secretary or Secretary of State, than the policy team for whom every new idea is one to be resisted or slowed down and who exist in a perpetual 'we've seen it all before' state of mind.

So what can be done to 'open up' Whitehall and to give ministers both a better service and a wider range of ideas and advice? Three things in our view, all of which are designed to improve on the range and quality of the support available to ministers.

First, ministers should be able to bring in more outside experts on short-term contracts without having to go in every case through the rules of 'fair and open' competition. In fairness to the Civil Service Commission there is already some scope for this within the rules that the Commission is willing to facilitate. And there would, of course, need to be limits to such recruitment to stop it becoming a way of undermining wholesale the normal route of competitive, merit-based entry into the civil service that we both continue to strongly support. But one could imagine, for example, every department being able to take on, say, up to half a dozen genuine experts at any one time, perhaps for periods of up to two years, without their having to be recruited through the normal competitive process. There would still need to be rules to guard against nepotism and conflicts of interest and those recruited would still have to abide by the normal civil service rules regarding political activities to prevent them from simply becoming additional special advisers by another route. But done properly this could lead to a significant increase in the breadth and depth of the expert advice available to ministers.

Secondly, and more radically, the steps which the present government has taken to allow departments, where ministers request it, to contract for the provision of policy advice and support in specific areas, from think tanks and outside bodies, could become as much the rule as the exception. In such instances there clearly needs to be a process of open and competitive tendering. These would be potentially valuable contracts and there could be no question of their being let on any kind of 'sweetheart' basis. There would almost certainly also need, akin to the position with consultancy contracts, to be some kind of pre-qualification stage where organisations and companies wanting to be able to bid for such contracts would have to demonstrate that they had the fundamental capability and experience to carry out such work. But assuming that such rules could be formulated this would potentially open up a market for policy advice and support to ministers to all those equipped to deliver it.

Where would this leave the classic Whitehall policy teams? And what would happen to the civil servants in them whose work was outsourced? In the latter case they would be in the same position as those undertaking delivery roles whose work is contracted out where there are now clear protocols for the handling of such situations, including in relation to TUPE – Transfer of Undertakings (Protection of Employment) regulations. In respect of the first question the truthful answer is probably that time would tell. Our suspicion is that many ministers would continue to regard the best of their in-house policy teams very highly. And there would undoubtedly be examples over time of policy advice being brought back in-house where outside organisations disappointed. But, overall, we believe that it would be healthy for the body politic, and for good governance, to open up Whitehall in this way and for a proportion of each department's 'policy' budget to be ring-fenced as a competitive tendering pot.

Thirdly, and somewhat less dramatically, we would both like to see much greater interchange between the Whitehall policy world and academia. By contrast with the United States it is striking how little time the average Whitehall policy-maker spends with the academic community in their field. There is no one magic bullet in this respect; secondments, exchanges, civil servants becoming visiting lecturers or professors, academics being invited regularly to hold policy seminars in Whitehall; all would have a role to play. But in the end what is probably needed is a change in culture in which Whitehall policy-makers regard academics as more natural allies in their quest to be able to offer the best support and advice to ministers and in which academics come to see Whitehall as a more natural customer for their work. And linked to the points we make above about the need for recruitment into the civil service to become more discipline and subject specific we would want to see the recruitment of academics into government, and indeed civil servants into academia, becoming – as it is in the United States – a much more normal and frequent career route.

The risk, which we recognise, is that the measures we propose above could lead to the gradual dismemberment of the Whitehall policy capability with as much or more to be lost than to be gained. But we have the confidence to believe that, after a period of adjustment, Whitehall would return the stronger and more confident, but alongside rather than instead of other respected sources of support to ministers.

CHAPTER 33

# RESPONSIBILITIES AND ACCOUNTABILITIES

NO ONE NOW BELIEVES IN the classic doctrine whereby ministers could be held accountable for every administrative act carried out by their department. If the DWP miscalculates Mrs Smith's pension the Secretary of State will normally never know let alone feel responsible. But suppose an IT error leads to a thousand Mrs Smiths having their pensions miscalculated. Is that still nothing to do with the Secretary of State? And suppose the same IT error leads to the miscalculation of over a million such pensions with a potential loss to the taxpayer running into hundreds of millions of pounds. Is that still nothing to do with the Secretary of State? And who in the last example should take the rap? The Secretary of State? The Permanent Secretary? The civil servant in direct charge of delivery?

The answer, as the example in the run-up to the 2012 Olympics of incoming passengers having to queue for hours to clear immigration controls at Heathrow shows, is that nobody knows. In that instance a very senior civil servant was effectively sacked and ministers were quick subsequently to blame their civil servants as well as their predecessors for the delays in clearing immigration, while the opposition was quick to blame them. The airlines blamed the government. The media blamed alternately bungling bureaucrats and meddling ministers. The public – as in 'they' need to sort this out – simply blamed 'them'.

Does any of this matter? Arguably this confusion has, like the weather, always existed and always gets resolved, somehow or other, in individual cases. And even if it does matter is it possible in practice to define responsibilities more clearly as between ministers and civil servants or is any such attempt simply doomed to failure?

In recent years those arguing that this confusion of responsibilities does matter, and is one of the causes of the UK not performing as well as it might, have tended to increase. In their important contribution to this issue ('Whitehall's Black Box' – IPPR, 2006) Ben Rogers and Guy Lodge argued forcefully that 'the inadequacies in Whitehall's system of Governance help explain its relatively weak record when it comes to performance'. They quoted one then Permanent Secretary (not the joint author of this book!) as saying:

> Although I think that the civil service is in the best shape that I have known it during my career, I would say that clarifying the roles of ministers and officials is the major unresolved constitutional question. It is a question that has been deliberately left untouched – the Pandora's Box that now needs opening.

Rogers and Lodge concluded that the government needed as a priority to recast the doctrine of ministerial accountability either by giving ministers the explicit power to hire and fire their top civil servants or by explicitly making ministers responsible for policy decisions and civil servants for operational ones on the lines of the changes in New Zealand where departmental heads were appointed and managed by a 'State Service Commissioner'.

More recently the Public Accounts Committee under its chair, Margaret Hodge, has become increasingly concerned that some of the senior civil servants appearing before it have been less than frank with the committee to the extent, in some cases, of seeking to keep facts from it. That has led the committee, in some instances controversially, to criticise individual civil servants publicly. This in turn has generated concerns amongst some of those at the top of the civil service that they are being left to carry the can without being able properly to defend themselves, or having any clear dividing line as to where their responsibilities and those of ministers begin and end. There is no doubt also that some senior people who have been brought in to the civil service from the private sector in recent years to deliver specific projects have left disillusioned by what they have seen as the constant moving of the political goalposts.

So what is our own view of this debate? First of all, we think it matters. Not being clear who is responsible for what in any organisation – let alone one as important as a government department – is a recipe for poor performance at best and total chaos at worst. We believe, as does the Public Accounts Committee and an increasing number of other commentators on government, that it is at least worth the effort to try to arrive at a clearer division of responsibilities.

But, secondly, we are – hopefully – not totally naive. It is unrealistic to believe, and would simply be wrong in any event, to think that on the day that there is a mass breakout from a high-security prison or a total meltdown of a major government IT system the Secretary of State concerned could ever tell the House of Commons that this was nothing to do with them but rather was totally the responsibility of the Permanent Secretary or of the Agency Chief Executive concerned. Were they to try their remaining political life could probably be measured in nano-seconds.

But, that said, we believe that there are some changes worth seriously considering. We put forward four.

First, we believe that it would be right to make explicit either in statute or in some other formal way that responsibility for the proper and effective management of government departments is a jointly held accountability of both the Secretary of State and the Permanent Secretary. While some might argue that this would be no more than a statement of the obvious we believe that it would, over time, condition behaviours on the part of both ministers and their senior civil servants. Put at its simplest neither could simply walk away claiming that it was the other's responsibility. And we believe that it would, over time, encourage better conversations between Secretaries of State and their Permanent Secretaries on the running of their departments.

Secondly, and linked to the above, we believe that the Public Accounts Committee should be under a duty to assess the contribution of both ministers and civil servants to the success or failure of particular programmes or policies and should be free to summon both the relevant Secretary of State and Permanent Secretary to appear jointly before it. That would get away from the unreality which pervades too many of the committee's hearings in which the committee has to take the policy in question as a given, no matter how ill-advised or unrealistic it may have been, and the Permanent Secretary has to shoulder the entire burden for its failure even though, privately, he or she may have advised against it from the very beginning. And if that were to be combined with a less confrontational, and more analytical, approach on the part of the PAC it could turn what is already an effective part of Parliament's architecture into an outstandingly successful one. Linked to this might be a published business case and risk assessment for every major programme of change, which could be opened to audit by the NAO and scrutiny by the PAC. On the side of the PAC, however, this would require it to be prepared to change its own approach and behaviours. No major programme will ever be free from risk or uncertainty. Grand-standing and headline-grabbing on the part of PAC members every time a minister or senior civil servant admits to any risk or uncertainty merely sends everyone back into their bunkers. If the NAO and the PAC want to be seen as one of the most serious and effective parts of the scrutiny system they have to be prepared to behave seriously themselves.

Thirdly, we would like to see ministers given a more explicit role in the selection of their most senior civil servant, i.e. the Permanent Secretary. This is sensitive and controversial territory – under much debate currently – and we would not want to see wholesale change from the present position in which the Civil Service Commission, overseeing the rules on 'fair and open competition', has a duty to ensure that senior civil service appointments are made on merit and merit alone. But that does not mean that there should be no role for the Secretary of State. The incumbent Secretary of State does already have a role in this respect in that their views are sought at the outset of the recruitment process on the key attributes that they want the next Permanent Secretary of their department to have, and in the fact that they do in the end have a right of veto, but not of selection, as to the actual appointment. But we would both go further and – broadly in line with the recent proposals from the Civil Service Commission – give an incumbent Secretary of State the right, if they wished to take it up, to choose between candidates where, but only where, a selection panel chaired by a Civil Service Commissioner – in practice that would normally be the First Civil Service Commissioner – had found two or more candidates for the role of Permanent Secretary to be both 'appointable' and of broadly equal merit. We believe that that would make in the end for better appointments and better Secretary of State/Permanent Secretary relationships. In putting forward this view we are conscious of the counter-argument that the Permanent Secretary is intended to be 'Permanent' while the Secretary of State could be reshuffled or fired the very next day. But that is no different from the position in any institution or boardroom where the idea, for example, of the chairman not being a key player in the appointment of the Chief Executive would simply not be understood.

Fourthly, and somewhat differently, we would like to see serious consideration given to a systematic re-creation of executive agencies. No one who has run such an agency – as one of us has – believes that they are the answer to every problem of accountability. And there have certainly been examples – the Prison Service in the time of Michael Howard as Home Secretary being perhaps the classic example

– where the limitations of the Agency model became very clear. Nevertheless it is arguably the model which has gone further than any other in the past quarter of a century in defining in a workable fashion the respective responsibilities of the Agency Chief Executive for delivery on the one hand and the responsible minister for policy on the other. It is also arguable that, in the great majority of cases, the Agency model has in practice helped deliver substantially improved service levels for citizens, by allowing management teams to concentrate fundamentally on delivery, while leaving ministers freer to concentrate on the policy that they wish to see delivered.

All government is in the end a fashion item and Executive Agencies have rather fallen out of fashion in recent years. Nevertheless, based on our own direct experience we believe that they still have a good deal to commend them and that they have got closer to providing a practical solution to the 'so who's in charge then?' question than any other model of which we are aware.

In putting forward these proposals we do not pretend that – either individually or collectively – they will completely remove all of the tensions over accountability which lie at the heart of our system of government. We do believe, however, that, if adopted, they would remove or reduce some of those tensions, possibly substantially. We believe that they are in this respect preferable to adopting the 'it's all too difficult' approach which has for too long tended to be the lowest common denominator in this particular debate.

CHAPTER 34

# TRUST

THIS MAY SEEM AN ODD title for the very final section of this short work. But having spent between us well over half a century in government we are both saddened by the degree to which our current political process is now routinely denigrated. Even if our advice is expressed at times in less than deeply academic terms, we hope that this short volume may indeed help some ministers to succeed better in delivering the policies on which they have been elected. And we hope that it will give the more general reader some sense of the huge range of issues and challenges with which a modern-day Secretary of State has to deal. But beyond all of that we hope that it may cause at least some of those who regard all politicians and all governments as beyond redemption and incapable of deserving their trust to reflect on whether this collective lack of respect for our political process is in fact merited.

If government was easy everyone would succeed. But it is not. All governments have perpetually to make choices between unpalatable alternatives in situations where there are less than ideal resources. All governments have to cope with the unexpected which cannot easily be foreseen. All governments have to manage expectations which cannot all be delivered. At times ministers and civil servants get it wrong and both should certainly be more ready to admit it when they do. At times – too many times – they allow short-term expediency to outweigh long-term necessity. But nonetheless – and irrespective of party – both of us believe on the basis of our own experience that the overwhelming majority of those engaged in the political process as MPs and ministers are seeking by their lights to do their best and to leave at least some elements of society better than they found them. We would like to see a restoration of trust in the political process not because it would make our politics healthier, though it would, but because we believe such trust to be merited. We hope that this volume, as well as hopefully having informed and entertained, may make a small contribution to that end.